HISTORY IN CA

D0489287

Fa

A

Shire Publications Ltd

Copyright © 1985 by Avril Lansdell. First published 1985; reprinted 1992. ISBN 0 85263 747 0.

Set in 11 on 11 point Times roman and printed in Great Britain by C. I. Thomas & Sons (Haverfordwest) Ltd, Press Buildings, Merlins Bridge, Haverfordwest, Dyfed.

Front cover: *A single carte in a Victorian style frame. This 1860s carte is from Miss Moffat's album (see plates 95 and 96).*

Title page: *A carte of the 1860s showing a woman in a crinoline-supported dress with a dropped shoulder line and braid-trimmed full sleeves, neat white cuffs and collar. Her cap, edged in several narrow lace frills, is tied beneath her chin and has long double lappets of lace which hang down to her waist. This style of indoor cap was very fashionable with married women in the 1840s, but by the 1860s was only worn by elderly women.*

Opposite: *A family group of the late 1850s: the mother in a tartan dress over a crinoline petticoat. She wears a white indoor cap tied beneath the chin. Father wears check trousers and a dark waistcoat and frock coat. Two of the little girls wear low-necked short-sleeved calf-length dresses with diagonally draped sashes. The child on the mother's lap wears a similar dress with a large handkerchief folded over her shoulders like a bib. The carte, by Draycott of Birmingham, Northampton and Walsall, has 'copied from another photograph' stamped along the left-hand edge. It may not have been printed as a carte until the 1890s.*

Contents

Cartes-de-visite were often taken on a very large plate and then each trimmed to 2¹/₄ by 3¹/₂ inches (57 by 89 mm). This untrimmed photograph shows a young woman in a wide-sleeved jacket worn over a plain crinoline-supported dress with collar and undersleeves of lace. She wears a brooch and a small pendant watch on a long chain. The picture was taken in the early 1860s and she has a fashionable hairstyle, parted in the middle, not quite covering the ears, with the back hair hidden by a snood, or net, made of silk chenille. In the finished carte the doors on each side, the floor boards and the top of the backcloth would all be trimmed away.

Introduction

Since the early 1970s an increasing general interest in all aspects of social history has led to a public awareness that the most commonplace objects can reveal a great deal about the way our ancestors lived and how they saw themselves. Victorian and Edwardian household utensils and the tools of local and rural industries are often the most popular specimens on display in museums, especially when they are arranged in room or workshop settings. Almost as popular in museums are clothes, although comparatively few clothes survive to represent the people who used the tools in the workshops so meticulously reconstructed.

The clothes that make up the museums' collections tend to be those of the middle and upper classes. Where working-class and artisans' clothes have survived they tend to be 'best' or 'special' wear — wedding clothes, christening gowns, mourning clothes, and others of the same kind. Many more women's clothes survive than those of men or children. To study the whole range of clothes worn in the past one must supplement research with pictorial sources as well as the actual garments, and for those interested in clothes from the middle of the nineteenth century onwards there exists the pictorial aid of photographs.

Today there is official recognition of the value of photographs, not only as records, but as objects in their own right. By 1971 the National Portrait Gallery had made a policy decision to collect photographs of both unknown and famous people as well as the paintings and drawings of the famous. In 1981 the Royal Photographic Society opened the National Centre of Photography in the Octagon at Bath, and in 1983 the Science Museum moved its main collection of photographs and photographic equipment to Bradford, where the National Museum of Photography is now open. The Victoria and Albert Museum has included a gallery on the history of photography and a photographic library as part of its new wing in Exhibition Road. The Imperial War Museum has a photographic library.

Between them these famous institutions own millions of photographs, the earliest dating from the 1840s. They cover all possible subjects. Even more millions are preserved in the combined collections of other national museums, provincial and local museums, record offices and libraries, private and family collections. Photographic libraries have been founded in sufficient numbers to warrant the publication of a directory of photographic collections in 1977. For students of costume these millions of photographs show — in all circumstances from the studio portrait to wartime journalistic photography — how people looked and what they wore.

This book is concerned with fashion as revealed in one type of Victorian photograph. This is the small, originally full-length portrait taken in a photographer's studio, mounted on pasteboard with the photographer's trade plate on the back, and known as a carte-de-visite.

1. *The front and back of a carte of 1865 showing the comparatively simple trade plate of the London Photographic Company backing a photograph of an elderly man wearing a single-breasted frock coat with wide lapels. This cut of coat was introduced from Paris in 1864. Although his coat is high fashion he wears it over a waistcoat with rolled lapels and a shirt with an old-fashioned high collar encircled with a dark cravat tied in a flat bow in front. The studio setting is typical of the early to mid 1860s.*

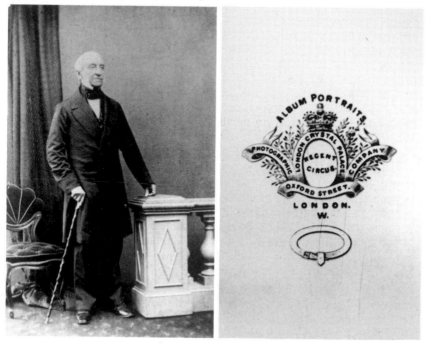

1. Popular photography

The first photographers

Although the world's first photograph was taken in the reign of George IV, the exposure needed by the bitumen of which it was made took eight hours. It was not until the reign of Queen Victoria, when Louis Daguerre and Henry Fox Talbot introduced the faster exposures of the daguerreotype and the calotype processes, using different methods, that any practical means of making portrait photographs was achieved. These early portraits date from 1841 but the exposure needed was still uncomfortably long and a number of head and body clamps were used by photographers to help their subjects maintain the required pose. This is one of the reasons why early Victorian photographs show such serious-faced people. It is much easier to stay still with the face relaxed than smiling. It is said that the phrase 'Watch the dicky-bird!' was first used in 1843 by a Parisian photographer, Mark Antonio Gaudin, who had a bird in a cage in his studio to attract the attention of a group of children he was photographing. Studio photographers have used the phrase ever since.

Daguerreotypes and calotypes were comparatively expensive. However, in 1851 Frederick Scott Archer invented the wet collodion process, which resulted in a glass negative that could be used again and again to produce a print and further copies. In 1854 another Parisian photographer, André Disdéri, patented a multi-lensed camera whereby eight small likenesses could be obtained on one large glass negative. The resulting contact print was cut up, the portraits were trimmed to 2¼ by 3½ inches (57 by 89 mm) and mounted on cards 2½ by 4 inches (63 by 102 mm). This was the usual size of a visiting card and the little photographs were promptly christened 'cartes-de-visite'.

Although they could be produced more cheaply than photographs taken by earlier methods, they were not, at first, very popular. However, five years later, in 1859, the French Emperor, Napoleon III, had his photograph taken by this process before departing for Italy at the head of his army. He distributed copies of the prints to his family and friends. Fashionable Paris followed his example; by 1861 Disdéri was the richest photographer in Paris and the craze for collecting cartes had begun. It was to spread all over Europe, and, although a larger format picture, the cabinet print, was popularised in 1866, the little carte-de-visite was to be the most common type of portrait photograph until almost the end of the nineteenth century.

Cartomania

The carte-de-visite was introduced to Britain in 1857. As in Paris, it was at first slow to catch the public's interest, but once the photographer J. E. Mayall had taken carte-de-visite portraits of the Royal Family — the Queen, Prince Albert and the royal children — in 1860, publishing them in 1861, its success was assured. If it was good enough for the Queen it was good enough for the British public, and so it proved. Photographers' studios were established in almost every street in every town in the British Isles. Photography and its attendant supplying industries boomed.

But not all these newly established photographers were skilled at their trade. Many of the back-street studios were run by men who were better at enticing passers-by with their promises than at taking good portraits. They cut their rates more and more to compete with each other, some even going so far as to offer 'Your likeness and a cigar for sixpence'. This would have been for a single carte.

The cartoonists in magazines such as *Punch* lampooned them mercilessly, featuring not only the persuasive powers of the photographer or his touts, but also the bad quality of his work, some of which faded within a fortnight. But along with the bad a great deal of good, reliable portrait photography was achieved at a very reasonable price, and these cartes have lasted to the present day as richly toned and as crisp and clean as when they were first taken. Prices for good, professional cartes-de-visite ranged from a guinea (£1.05) for a dozen prints, with a range of small variations in the pose, down to half a guinea in the vast

2 (opposite, upper). *Two cartes from a set portraying a young woman about 1869 or 1870. From 1865 a square 'yoke' effect to the top of a bodice was very popular. This yoke was usually defined by fringing or braid, and the style was fashionable into the early 1870s. By the late 1860s the crinoline had passed the peak of favour and many women had abandoned it in favour of the crinolette (a petticoat that had hoops only at the back) or the bustle. This woman is wearing a bustle. Her back hair is braided, and caught up to the crown of her head. The studio setting is typical of the late 1860s with its curtain, table, chair and painted window with a country scene seen through it.*

3 (opposite, lower). *Two cartes from the mid 1880s. The studio setting is much more elaborate, although it still has a curtain and table. The Chinese screen, peacock feather fan and oriental jug are typical of the fussier settings of the 1880s. The girl wears small, metal-rimmed spectacles, she favours the drawn-back hairstyle of the 1870s rather than the fringe so popular in the 1880s. Her dress is made of gauzy material with a silk stripe in it and, for all its apparent looseness, it is mounted on a firm lining. The skirt consists of tiers of pleated frills under an overskirt that is drawn up at the left hip rather than at the back. Her bodice has the three-quarter length sleeves ending in a lace frill that became fashionable from 1883. She wears a wide leather belt that contrasts with the thin fabric of her dress. The upstanding white collar, probably tacked into the neckband of her bodice, is edged with a small 'pie-crust' frill.*

4 (above, left). *One of John Mayall's cartes of Queen Victoria and Prince Albert, taken in 1860 and published as part of an album in August 1861. Later the various pictures were reproduced and sold separately. This carte, published by Marion and Company, would have been one of a run of several thousand which were probably sold for a shilling or one shilling and sixpence each. The Queen was never a fashion leader. Her dress — with its horizontal trimmings on the skirt and wide sleeves with white undersleeves — and her hairstyle, parted in the middle and drawn down to cover her ears, are reminiscent of the fashions of the mid 1850s. This carte shows Albert standing beside the seated Queen. In many royal pictures he is the seated figure, while Victoria stands beside him. He wears a dark suit of trousers, buttoned waistcoat and an open frock coat over a white shirt and stiffened upstanding collar held in place with a dark stock tied in a bow, the forerunner of the bow tie.*

5 (above, right). *An early carte by John Mayall. In an elaborate studio setting a middle-aged woman poses for her photograph. Her clothes are of the early 1860s: an untrimmed, vertically striped dress over a crinoline petticoat, worn under a short jacket trimmed with braid. She is more stylishly dressed than the Queen, in plate 4. Her hairstyle, however, was fashionable when she was younger, in the late 1840s, with its dangling side curls and the back hair coiled into a bun. She has changed her clothes with the times, but not her hairstyle.*

majority of established provincial photographers. Cheaper ones could be had and even some of these have lasted well enough, if somewhat faded now, to give an accurate picture of the clothes of all social classes of the period, for in many of these cartes the face of the sitter has faded more than the clothes. The back of the carte was used as the photographer's trade plate, and these, as time went by, became works of art in themselves. On them the photographers listed their achievements or their patrons; some included their prices. Many offered copies or enlargements 'up to life-size' and these could be coloured in oil or water colour.

Others offered to copy old photographs, and some cartes bear stamped on the face 'Copied from an old photograph'. Sometimes these cartes show people in the fashions of the 1840s or 1850s. Many women helped their husbands or brothers to run photographic studios, often carrying on the business alone in later years after the death of their partners.

In 1861 there were one hundred and sixty-eight portrait studios in London, twenty-seven of them in Regent Street alone, most of them specialising in cartes-de-visite. By 1866 there were two hundred and eighty-four such studios. The originator of the carte-de-visite, Disdéri, himself opened two studios in London in 1867, one in Brooke Street, off Hanover Square, and the other in Hereford Lodge, Old Brompton. This second studio had closed by 1870, but the Brooke Street Studio continued to take photographs until 1894.

6 (below, left). *A cartoon published in Punch on 29th September 1860.*
7 (below, right). *An example of a carte in which the base of the clamp stand can be seen behind the ankles of a boy about nine or ten years old. He wears a collarless jacket (above which his collar and tie show), a waistcoat and long trousers. The photographer was E. L. Bridge of Deal, Kent, and the picture has '1867' written on the back.*

"STEP IN, AND BE DONE, SIR!"

London was not the only place where photographers flourished. In the 1860s Horatio Nelson King, a photographer in Bath, reported that his local carte-de-visite sales were between sixty and seventy thousand a year. Similar figures probably applied in other large provincial cities.

Backgrounds and balustrades

The carte-de-visite was at first a formal photograph designed only to present the likeness of the subject, but soon a studio setting became fashionable as photographers vied with each other for trade. These settings, and the 'props' that went with them, can help to date the cartes, for they changed over the decades.

In the mid 1860s a classical column, a balustrade and a heavy curtain were used, sometimes with a table or writing desk and a chair. Fans or books were useful props for adults who did not know what to do with their hands. Small children were stood on chairs; these varied from plain kitchen chairs to velvet parlour chairs according to the status of the photographer. Some studios kept toys for children to play with and the same toys appear in pictures of unrelated children. By the mid 1870s very elaborate chairs with padded backs, on which the subjects — especially women and children — leaned, were favoured. A substitute for such a chair was a padded 'rest' like a very elaborate lectern. These appear in cartes into the 1880s.

In the late 1860s a painted window with a country scene glimpsed through it became popular. In the 1870s the window disappeared and large rural backcloths were used by many

8 (opposite). *The back of a carte taken in the 1860s (top left). The trade plate contains only the name and address of the studios in a small and simple design.*

9 (top right). *By the 1870s the designs were becoming more ornate. J. W. Thomas had been established nearly twenty years when the carte of which this is the back was taken: he had already produced over fifty thousand negatives. The design has spread to cover the whole of the back of the carte and incorporates the Royal Arms.*

10 (bottom left). *In the 1880s the elaboration was at its height, and as much information and decoration as possible was packed on to the back of the carte, including pictures of the medals won by the photographer at various exhibitions up and down the country. The printing of carte backs was often done in France or Germany and sent over to England. This carte back was printed in Paris. The photographer took the picture in plate 70.*

11 (bottom right). *1890s carte backs were 'artistic', some with drawings of women in 'classical' dress which still contrived to be fashionable (see plate 78). Many of the mounts for 1890s cartes were dark with the drawing and lettering in white or gold. As in the 1880s the photographers put as much information as possible on the cartes, listing their branches and the notable people they had photographed. Hellis and Sons, who photographed the little girl in plates 107 and 108, had also photographed the exotically named Akbaloddowla, ex King of Oude.*

photographers. These were supplied ready-made for the trade and the same backcloth can be found in several studios around Britain. Stiles, fences or garden furniture were placed in front of these backcloths. In the summer these rustic studio props were sometimes taken into the photographer's garden. Boats or boat rigging were used for pictures of small boys in sailor suits, while small girls were posed with baskets of flowers from the 1870s onward.

In the 1880s the balustrade returned. The painted backcloth was still used, especially if the photographer had an ordinary (penny-farthing) bicycle and a set of cycling clothes to loan to sporting minded young men. Chinese or Japanese screens appear in cartes of the 1880s and some interior settings became very elaborate. By the 1890s interiors with potted palms or mirrors were in vogue, or very artificial garden settings. At seaside towns some photographers had 'studios' actually on the beach or at the base of a cliff, with rocks or the wooden quoins as seats or props.

The indoor studio settings were, however, the gimmicks of the trade. Many photographers preferred plain backgrounds for the whole of the period in which cartes were in favour. In these cases, only the clothes of the people portrayed can give any indication of the year in which the picture was taken.

12 (opposite, top left). *A carte of the mid 1860s showing a painted window with a country scene. (Note the ridge of the hoop of the sitter's petticoat showing through the folds of her skirt.)*

13 (opposite, top right). *A carte of the 1870s with rustic furniture in front of a scenic background. The man wears a morning coat with velvet collar and cuffs, a striped double-breasted waistcoat with a long watch chain, and trousers with cross pockets in front. (Note the turndown flaps on his trouser pockets, and the heavy leather belt round his waist).*

14 (opposite, bottom left). *A small boy in a sailor suit in the 1880s is given a ship's mast and rigging to 'climb'. Sailor suits were so common for boys' wear that this sort of nautical setting could be found in photographic studios far from the sea. This carte was taken in the studio of Helsden and Son, in Hertford.*

15 (opposite, bottom right). *A young woman of the 1890s is posed in a fanciful 'garden' setting. It is much heavier in effect than the 1870 setting. (Note the balloon shape of her upper sleeves, which date this carte to 1895.) Taken in the studio of John Hicks in Horsham.*

16 (left). *This couple was photographed in Norwich about 1862. They wear informal clothes, the man in light trousers and a darker waistcoat and morning coat, the woman in a crinoline-supported dress, the low-set sleeves of which are very wide and puffed at the top. This was a fashion that became popular between 1862 and 1865. As her skirt is evenly gathered all round below her tight-fitting bodice with its sloping braid decoration, the earlier date is indicated. Her hair reveals only the lobes of her ears and is taken back in a soft wave. It is not as severe as the style of the 1850s but it is not taken off the face in the fashion of the mid 1860s. Men in the 1860s seldom wore full beards until near the end of the decade. This man has a fringe beard, but no moustache.*

17 (right). *A more formal photograph of a slightly older couple, taken about 1866. In this carte the man wears a frock coat over light trousers. He is far more self-conscious than the man in the earlier photograph. His wife, too, sits rigidly upright, holding a letter in her lap. Her bodice is cut in similar style to the other woman and her sleeves are set into the same low shoulder line but they are plain, trimmed with braid at the shoulder and wrist. Her skirt shows how the fashions have changed for it has no gathers across the front, and all the fullness has moved to the back. The vertical lines of braid on the front of her skirt give an optical illusion of a double skirt, hinting at fashions to come. This woman's hair is drawn back exposing her ears and her back hair is held in a snood. The woman's jewellery is interesting. She has a brooch at the neck of her dress, a small pendant on a short chain, and a watch in a special watch pocket set into the waistband of her skirt. The watch is attached to a long chain which is fastened to the middle button of her bodice. The man has a moustache and very long sidewhiskers, leaving his chin clean-shaven.*

2. The fashionable carte

Fashion and Victorian society

The fashions revealed by the cartes-de-visite date from the late 1850s. They cover all strata of society and show that by the middle of the nineteenth century some of the old class distinction, of dress at least, was beginning to disappear. It was said at the time that 'the distinction in dress between the higher and middle classes is, in many respects, nullified'. By the 1850s a desire to be fashionable had penetrated right down the social scale. 'The housemaid now dresses better — finer at all events — than her mistress did twenty years ago, and it is almost impossible to recognise working people when in their Sunday best,' wrote an observer in 1858. The cartes-de-visite bear this out, for it is not always easy to place the figures in the photographs in their level in the social scale.

Social conventions are easier to see in the cartes than social scale. Mourning played a great part in all Victorian women's clothes. The texture of black crepe shows up well in many cartes-de-visite and the amount of crepe indicated which stage the mourning had reached.

The quality of the fabrics may have distinguished the classes, but because of the widespread custom of passing on clothes of all kinds by the upper classes (and those who followed their lead) as soon as a new fashion appeared even this small distinction was blurred as time went by. Only if a photograph is very definitely annotated can one judge how new the clothes are, and so, perhaps, place it in the social scale: the poorer the wearer the more out of date their clothes are likely to be. Age, too, can confuse the issue. Many older people preferred the clothes and hairstyles that were fashionable or conventional at their prime of life to the new-fangled fashions adopted by a younger generation.

In addition to the straightforward style, cut and colours of clothes a great many subtleties have to be taken into account when attempting to date photographs simply by what the sitter is wearing. This fact makes the subject more interesting. Among these subtleties are the hairstyles, hats and watch-chains of the men and the trimming, accessories, jewellery, hats and hairstyles of the women and children.

1858 to 1870

At the end of the 1850s and during the early 1860s women wore their hair very simply. A centre parting was almost universal, with the hair brought down over the ears (where it was sometimes puffed out) and then turned back to be wound in a small bun or chignon at the nape of the neck. By the middle of the 1860s the ears were almost always exposed. The hair was still parted in the centre but an even newer style took it straight back off the forehead to be wound in a chignon much larger than that of the 1850s. The chignon, often supplemented with added false hair, climbed steadily up the back of the head during the 1860s.

Most of the women in the earliest cartes wear a crinoline. This was a framework made of hoops of whalebone or steel, worn under the dress skirt and top petticoat, holding them out from the wearer's legs. The crinoline took the place of the many layers of petticoats used to achieve a dome-shaped skirt in earlier decades and was much cooler and more comfortable. However it needed care in its management if it was not to swing revealingly when walking or get in the way when sitting. Even though the masculine world thought the crinoline illogical and funny (crinolines were caricatured in *Punch* as much as photographers), it remained popular. The wide skirt made every waist look smaller, and corsets in the 1850s and 1860s were not laced as tightly as they had been in the 1830s and 1840s, or as tightly as

18 (opposite, top left). *A middle aged woman posing for a Manchester photographer in a fashionable dress of 1860. Close examination of this carte reveals that the dress was a fine striped taffeta (a very fashionable fabric in the 1860s) for the stripes show up in the shadows. The dress, worn over a crinoline petticoat, is lavishly trimmed with braid in a large 'Greek key' pattern. The sleeves are set into a low line and flare from the armhole. Gauzy undersleeves show beneath them. These undersleeves were called 'engageants' and were separate garments which covered the forearms from just above the elbow to the wrist. They were usually gathered into a small frilled cuff at the wrist which buttoned tight. At the elbow they were gathered with a drawstring or elastic. The woman's hair is parted in the middle and taken over her ears in a roll which is probably pinned into a small bun at the back. Over her hair she wears a dark veil which hangs down her back.*

19 (opposite, top right). *Most dresses of the 1860s were made with a separate skirt and bodice. Many were made with two bodices, one high-necked and long-sleeved for the day, the other low-necked and short-sleeved for evening wear. This carte shows a young woman of the early 1860s in her evening dress and reveals how the clever use of a net yoke gives the appearance of a very low-necked off-the-shoulder line while remaining very decorously high-necked.*

20 (opposite, bottom left). *This carte, published about 1862, shows the voluminous cape that had been in use since the early nineteenth century. It was to remain a useful garment until almost the end of the century. But even in the 1860s it has an old-fashioned look to it, especially when seen with a bonnet that was high fashion in 1848-50. Although these clothes could have been worn in the 1860s, especially by an older woman, it is possible that this picture, like that on page 3, was copied from an earlier photograph of the 1850s.*

21 (opposite, bottom right). *Much more fashionable is this plain crinoline-supported dress of the mid 1860s shown in a carte by John Mayall. The woman wears an 1850s hairstyle associated with middle-aged women, but tops it with a very fashionable little summer hat with streamers hanging down the back. Her oblong lace shawl is a decorative accessory, designed for show, not warmth, and is the type of garment that would have been chosen by a fashion-conscious matron rather than a young woman.*

22. *A pair of cartes showing either husband and wife or father and daughter, taken in the Cramb Brothers' studio, Glasgow. The studio setting is mid 1860s and the clothes of the couple are comfortable rather than highly fashionable. The woman wears a crinoline-supported, braid-trimmed 'tartan' silk dress with a small white collar and brooch. Her sleeves are in the style known as 'pagoda' sleeves and she wears white 'engageants' beneath them. Her hair is neatly parted and covers her ears. The back of her carte is inscribed 'To Mrs McLean with fondest love'. The man wears light trousers, a dark waistcoat and frock coat, a white shirt and a bow tie. He carries a rolled umbrella and has a fringe of beard but no moustache. On the back of his picture is written 'To Mrs McLean with kind regards'.*

they would be again in the 1880s and 1890s.

The crinoline was at its widest in the early 1860s. By 1865 it began to shrink, first altering its shape from a dome to a half dome, flat in the front and with all the fullness taken to the back. Many women abandoned the crinoline after 1867, relying on petticoats, pads and a tighter-laced corset to achieve the fashionable shape. The vast skirts of the early 1860s became overskirts, looped up at the sides and bunched out behind by the end of the decade, heralding the bustle dresses of the 1870s.

Above the crinoline-supported wide skirts the dress bodice was cut to mould the figure. A modest high neck for day wear, with a little collar, made an ideal setting for a pretty brooch, while the wide long sleeves were set in to the bodice low down on the shoulder line, to achieve the sloping shoulder that was the ideal of the early 1860s. The seam was to rise during the decade until, by 1870, the sleeve was set in to the bodice on the point of the shoulder. Epaulettes, or braid trimmings on the tops of the sleeves, were popular all through the decade.

The cut of the bodice (usually a separate garment from the skirt) and the low-set sleeve effectively prevented women from making vigorous arm movements. Quietness and stillness in women were considered to add to their charms, and the length of time needed for a photographic exposure enabled most women to give this impression. Many dresses of the 1860s had two bodices, a high-necked, long-sleeved one for day wear, while a low-necked, short-sleeved bodice that looked as if it were about to fall off the shoulders of the wearer could be substituted for evening wear with the same skirt. However, more cartes-de-visite show a

23. A pair of cartes taken in Isaac Wilde's studio in Blackpool about 1866-7. The young man, who has a beard and no moustache, wears a morning suit. The edges of his coat are bound with a lighter braid. His collar is of the 'stand-up' type and he wears a knotted tie. The young woman wears a plain dress with a 'yoke' effect to the bodice, outlined in a fringed braid. This same fringed braid also decorates her sleeves and was a very popular fashion feature in the mid to late 1860s. Her skirt is box-pleated into the waistband with a plain panel across the front. Her hat sits uncompromisingly on the top of her head and has a small veil hanging behind. The hat is probably made of velvet, gathered and ruched into a 'pork pie' shape, and decorated in front with artificial flowers. She wears no wedding ring, so this pair of cartes may well have been of a brother and sister, rather than husband and wife.

daytime bodice than an evening one.

Girls wore wide, crinoline-supported skirts like their mothers, although their skirts were only knee or calf length according to their age. Little girls' bodices were more like adult evening dress with low necks and short sleeves.

Very small boys wore dresses like the little girls or sturdier but still similar tunics, not over crinoline petticoats but over elaborate lace-trimmed drawers that showed below the dress. Some dresses for small boys had pleated skirts like kilts, and matching jackets. Before they reached the age of six or seven years boys were put into knickerbockers and jackets, often decorated with braid. The knickerbockers were just below the knee in length and could be straight at this point or set into a band. This basic suit for boys was to continue in fashion almost to the end of the century, along with the alternative of the more casual sailor suit, which replaced the jacket by a serge blouse with a square-cut collar tied in front, reminiscent of an able seaman's uniform. As they grew older, boys were clothed in long trousers and short jackets, very like a

24 (opposite, top left). *This very fashion-conscious young woman of the mid 1860s was photographed in the Kingston upon Thames studio of Ayliffe, who described himself as a 'photographic artist'. She wears a crinoline-supported box-pleated skirt, a white blouse and a flowing jacket, which is trimmed with braid to match the trimming on her skirt, and carries a wide-brimmed straw hat. The fashion image is that popularised by the young Princess of Wales, who married Queen Victoria's eldest son in 1863. Alexandra, Princess of Wales, wore jackets over skirts and blouses. They were both practical and pretty, and many women followed her example. She also wore the 'off the ears' hairstyle, and her hats, like this one, were widely copied.*

25 (opposite, top right). *A woman in an outdoor walking dress, late 1860s. Her skirt is flat in front, with all the fullness taken to the back where it is lengthened into a train which could be caught up in the hand to clear it from the ground when necessary. Her double-breasted jacket, cut like a man's reefer coat, was considered very daring when it was first worn. Her 'pork-pie' hat is worn tipped over her forehead and her hair is braided up into a high chignon at the back. Her accessories are neat leather gloves and rolled umbrella.*

26 (opposite, bottom left). *This young woman of the late 1860s wears a very fashionable double skirt with a slight train. She wears a crinolette or half hoops under her skirt at the back. The shorter top skirt is made up of shaped panels, the seams being gathered up at their lower edges to form swagged folds in the fabric at the back. Her lighter-coloured bodice (which may well be a blouse, tucked into her skirt, for these became fashionable in the 1860s) still retains the style of the mid 1860s bodices with its low-set bishop sleeves trimmed with braid or tatted lace at wrist and shoulder seams. The join between skirt and blouse is covered by a belt which has a diamond-shaped panel at the front and was known as a 'Swiss' belt. These were to remain in fashion for wear with skirts and blouses until the 1890s. Her hairstyle is very youthful and elegant, with the sides rolled above her ears and the back hair confined in a net trimmed with flowers and lace. She carries a folded fan.*

27 (opposite, bottom right). *At the turn of the 1860s and 1870s, this woman's tartan silk dress shows how much the fashions had changed in ten years. She wears a small bustle under her skirt at the back. The dress is trimmed with small frills of the same fabric and with bands of velvet ribbon. The neckline is a gentle vee-shape, the sleeves are set in at the natural point of the shoulder. Her hair is taken back off her face and made into a large roll, possibly augmented with false hair. It is set off with a lacy ornament and she wears drop ear-rings.*

28 (opposite, top left). *A young woman and child photographed in 1860. The woman wears a plain dress, with bishop sleeves, over a crinoline petticoat. The dress is trimmed only by a band of darker material round the hem and by the buttons right down the front. It could have been made of soft cashmere wool or taffeta. With it she wears a small white collar and a brooch at the neck. Her hairstyle is that of the late 1850s with a centre parting and the hair puffed out over the ears. The little girl wears a mid calf-length dress (probably with a short crinoline petticoat under it) and a loose coat fastened at the neck. Her dress is decorated with braid in the popular 'Greek key' pattern (see plate 18) and she wears white socks and ankle-strap shoes. The photograph was taken in the studio run by Mr and Mrs Dixon in Lymington.*

29 (opposite, top right). *The boy photographed here is possibly seven or eight years old. His suit has long trousers and his jacket has a small collar, above which his shirt collar shows. His waistcoat copies those of adult men. Both he and his sister carry hats with broad ribbons round them, so the photograph was probably taken in the summer. The girl's hat is a pale straw and the boy's dark hat could be straw or felt. The girl wears a low-necked, mid calf-length dress trimmed with buttons and braid. She wears ankle boots, which were equally popular for boys or girls. Her hairstyle is very adult and fashionable with its neat roll of turned-under curls at the back of her head. Note the narrow ribbon and medallion at her neck. This was fashionable for adult evening dress and small girls' clothes tended to copy adults' evening dress. This carte was taken in Plymouth about 1865.*

30 (opposite, bottom left). *Three sisters photographed in Portsea in the mid 1860s. It was common at this time to dress sisters alike, regardless of age or build. These three girls are probably wearing the same colour, but there are distinct variations in the styles of their clothes and these variations relate to their ages. The oldest girl is wearing an adult-length skirt over a crinoline. The two younger girls are wearing the above-the-ankle skirts of the young teenager. (Compare them with the slightly shorter-length skirts worn by the younger girls in plates 28 and 29.) The girl on the left seems to be wearing hoops under her skirt, unlike her sister on the right. All three dresses have the fashionable low shoulder line, two of them with braid trimming. All the girls wear broad belts with large buckles. Like most 1860s dresses, their bodices button down the front. The youngest girl, with the muff, wears her hair loose and held back with a band. (These bands were later to be known as 'Alice' bands, after Tenniel's drawings for Lewis Carroll's story of 'Alice in Wonderland' which showed Alice wearing such a hairstyle and band.) The two older girls have braided their hair or taken it up in a small bun at the back. The girl on the left has a ribbon in her hair, which hangs over her left shoulder.*

31 (opposite, bottom right). *The back of this carte, taken at the studio of J. Gilchrist in Edinburgh, is inscribed 'Flo, Berta and nurse 1868'. The two little girls are dressed alike in dresses with short sleeves trimmed with braid. The bottoms of their skirts are also braid-trimmed. Both wear white pinafores over the top of their dresses. The older girl wears an 'Alice' band, but the younger girl has hair that is still too short for a band. The nurse wears a dress with its sleeve-tops puffed in the way that was fashionable between 1862 and 1864 (see plate 16). The bodice has a square 'yoke' on the front outlined in braid. Her sleeves have white cuffs and there is the edge of a white under-band showing at the neck of her dress. She may well be wearing a full-length apron, over the front of her dress, made of the same fabric as her skirt. If not, her skirt has deep box-pleats at each side. Her hair is centre-parted and is taken above her ears to the back, where it is braided and the braids looped across the back of her head.*

junior version of naval officers' uniform (the 'midshipman' style), or in trousers and morning coats or lounge jackets like those worn by adult men.

Formal dress for men in 1860 consisted of trousers, shirt, waistcoat and a frock coat, which had a fitted waist and was then slightly flared to the knee. This steadily went out of fashion and was replaced by the morning coat, which had the front part below the waist cut away in a sloping line. For informal wear gentlemen were adopting the lounge suit with its shorter jacket. Lower middle-class men and artisans rapidly adopted the lounge suit as best wear. In the early 1860s most men were still wearing light-coloured trousers with a jacket in a darker colour. (This had been fashionable since the start of the century.) Waistcoats were in a different fabric again, usually darker than the trousers.

The cartes-de-visite cannot show the colours, since they are, unless hand-painted afterwards, monochrome — usually sepia-toned — photographs. However, they clearly show the relationship of the tones of the colours. Lounge suits were usually, but not always, a matching set of trousers, waistcoat and jacket; when matching, they were often made in checked fabric and were known as a 'suit of dittos'. On plain trousers a raised side seam, or a contrast braid sewn over the side seam, was fashionable. As well as the morning coat and the lounge jacket, many variations of short double-breasted 'reefer' or 'pea' jackets were worn, particularly in the lower middle and labouring classes.

32 (opposite, top left). *This little boy, probably three years old, was photographed in Plymouth in the early 1860s. He wears a dress made in a low-necked, short-sleeved style that would have been equally suitable for a boy or girl. The frilly drawers showing beneath it mark him out as a boy, as does his very short hair. The dress has a full skirt trimmed with velvet ribbon and the short sleeves are gathered into the low armhole and then ruched vertically to make them shorter. This was probably a summer dress in a bright (possibly red) cashmere fabric. He wears white socks and front-laced ankle boots.*
33 (opposite, top right). *This little boy was called Charlie. He was four years old in August 1867 when this carte was taken by Harry Emmens of Liverpool. The carte was inscribed and sent to 'Grandpapa Barker', who must have lived abroad, for the word 'England' is added after 'Liverpool' on the trade plate at the back of the carte. Charlie has been promoted out of dresses and wears knickerbockers, a shirt, waistcoat and a collarless jacket over which his shirt collar is turned down. His outfit is finished with a real bow tie, long-stockings and ankle length boots. This carte was hand-coloured.*
34 (opposite, bottom left). *A teenager wearing light trousers and a double-breasted 'chesterfield' type coat which could serve as a jacket or overcoat. Although it cannot be seen he would have worn a waistcoat similar to those worn by the younger boys above. His name, 'Pat Dillon,' is written on the back of the carte, taken by Adolphus Wing of London.*
35 (opposite, bottom right). *A young man in his early twenties, in a lounge suit made from one fabric. It looks deceptively modern, but the deep cuffs to the sleeves and the over-long trousers with no front crease date it to the late 1860s. He carries a straw hat with a dark ribbon, and wears a watch in his waistcoat pocket, its chain passed through the second buttonhole on his waistcoat.*

36 (above left). *A middle-aged man in a frock coat, fastened by only the top button, over a tweed waistcoat and matching trousers. Note that these have neither turn-ups nor front crease. His facial hair is typical of the 1860s for, although long, it is not a complete set of whiskers as his chin is clean-shaven. It gives the impression of a beard with a centre parting.*
37 (above right). *A man in a morning coat and matching waistcoat with light trousers. He wears a 'four in hand' tie (knotted in the modern way with a stud pin set in the knot) round an upstanding collar. This carte was taken in the very elegant studio of Edward Reeves, about 1868. Edward Reeves had opened this studio in Lewes, Sussex, in 1858 and the studio has passed through four generations of the same family of photographers. It is still open and is being run by the great-grandson of the founder, using the original Victorian daylight studio. The complete collection of over one hundred thousand negatives from the 1850s to the present day has been retained; the bulk of those of the nineteenth century are now in the care of the Sussex Archaeological Society at the Barbican House Museum in Lewes.*
38 (opposite, left). *A very smart young man photographed in 1865. He wears a frock coat with a velvet collar and deep lapels (the Parisian style, see plate 1). His trousers have a broad dark stripe down each outer seam. His shirt has a soft turn-down collar and he also wears a 'four-in-hand' tie. His top hat is straight-sided and the medium height which became fashionable in 1865.*
39 (opposite, right). *A Victorian 'swell' in matching trousers, waistcoat and morning coat. Matching clothes like this were known as 'a suit of dittos'. Note the slanting pockets in the trousers and the braid binding the edges of his coat and waistcoat. This braid also defines a deep cuff on each sleeve. His tie is a small bow tie, possibly made up and pinned on; his collar is a soft 'turn-down'. His top hat is medium height, but has the curving sides that became popular in the late 1860s. His facial hair is in the style known as 'Dundreary whiskers' after 'Lord Dundreary', a comic stage character of the 1860s.*

1870 to 1880

There are two immediately obvious differences between the cartes-de-visite of women in the 1860s and the 1870s. The first is the more elaborate hairstyles, and the second is the changing shape of the dress, which became much more tightly fitting than in the days of the crinoline. The skirts of the early 1870s were draped and folded, trimmed with frills, ribbons, buttons and/or fringing. Most skirts were double or were trimmed to simulate a long skirt worn under a shorter overskirt which was caught up and held out at the back by a bustle pad or a half crinoline or 'crinolette', attached to the back of the waist under the skirts. Bodices were still very simple in shape but the sleeves were set into the bodice higher on the shoulder line, and the epaulettes disappeared. The photographs of necklines in the 1870s show more variety, as they could be high or cut low in a vee-shape or square. Modesty insertions, scarves and jabots were common.

40 (left). *There are several differences between cartes-de-visite of the 1860s and 1870s. In the 1870s 'half' or 'three-quarters' length portraits began featuring in the cartes. The 1860s cartes are almost always full-length seated or standing figures. In the 1870s the camera began to move in closer. Another most noticeable difference is in the hairstyles of the women. It was said that, in the 1870s, one firm was turning out two tons of artificial hair a week. This hair was used in padding out women's heads. Their hair always left the ears uncovered, but it was then built up on the head in coiled tresses, plaits or curls covering the crown. Sometimes cascades of curls hung down the back. Photographed in the early 1870s, this young woman (left) from Liverpool has strained her hair back over her temples but has then built it up into a luxuriant froth of curls descending her back. The style is accented by the rose worn in the hair. Much jewellery and many ornaments were worn in the 1870s and this girl wears long ear-rings. Dresses were trimmed with frills and flounces, lace and velvet ribbons. The high neck of this girl's dress (possibly a late 1860s dress with new trimmings) is softened by a frilled scarf fastened with a pendant hanging from a bow of ribbon. The yoke of her dress is outlined by a lace frill.*

41 (right). *Later in the decade hairstyles became more severe as did the general cut of dresses. This woman (right) has swept her own hair back over pads of false hair to build it up at the temples. It is made into a chignon at the back where it is finished with a ribbon bow. In the parting at the front she wears a large ornament that seems vaguely Egyptian. She is also wearing dark ear-rings, probably jet, and a carved jet chain around her neck, hanging over the lace jabot at her throat. Her sleeves are fairly wide at the wrist and are trimmed with lace and braid. The carte was taken by Alfred Harman, who was to be the founder of the firm of Ilford, and who at this time had photographic studios in Surbiton and Peckham.*

By the late 1870s even the bustle had gone, at least in high fashion. Fashion plates of the time show that the ideal dress fitted the body tightly from shoulders to hips, while the narrow, swathed skirts shackled the legs so that walking must have been extremely difficult. The cartes-de-visite show many practical variations on this style, in which a close-fitting hip-length jacket was worn above an earlier fashion of skirt while the bustle seems to have slipped almost to the knees. In some photographs the 'jacket' is even longer than hip-length, making a princess-line dress with no seam at the waist. Even in this style, though, the back of the skirt is draped up over a longer underskirt. Surviving dresses of the late 1870s reveal that tapes were sewn inside skirts so that they could be tied back behind the body in order to hold the front close to the figure. All the drapery and trimmings then cascaded down to a long but narrow train that could be lifted from its end by one hand without revealing the legs. Such dresses would have been worn only by the class of woman who had servants to do the work. Women who were themselves active, in whatever sphere, wore dresses that were narrow, but without trains.

Girls' dresses were almost as complicated as those of their mothers; only the length was different and much shorter. Even so, double skirts were common in the early 1870s. Sisters, even if widely spaced in age, were often dressed alike, or in variations on a fashion theme in the same fabric and colour. By the middle of the decade the princess-line dress was much in favour for young women and girls. It was worn even by toddlers. While very small girls did not wear bustles they often had a small pad at the back, below the waist, to give a fashionable line to the dress. Girls' dresses were trimmed with ruched frills, as were those of adult women. The tightly fitting dress and the tied-back skirt, however, were not worn by small girls.

Little boys wore much the same clothes as they had in the 1860s. The dresses were, perhaps, discarded for the knicker-bocker suits at a slightly earlier age, and the sailor suit in all its variations became more and more common. As the decade went on the knickerbockers lost their fullness and their kneebands to become simple trousers cut off at the knee. Double-breasted reefer jackets were worn with these, or the newer Norfolk jacket, which had pleats from the shoulders at front and back and was worn belted.

Norfolk jackets were also available for men from the mid 1870s. They were at first called Norfolk shirts and, made in flannel, were worn for sports. Later they were made in serge or suiting materials and were then regarded as jackets, still largely worn on sporting or country occasions. The majority of middle-class men still wore the morning coat and trousers for their everyday attire, although the lounge suit was gaining ground for leisure time, and for everyday wear (when not at work) among the artisan class. The frock coat was for formal wear only or was worn by elderly men who had worn it all their lives and found it more comfortable than other styles. From 1876 waistcoats matched either the morning coat or the lounge jacket and the days of fancy waistcoats, for normal wear, were over.

The value of a collection of cartes-de-visite to the costume historian is shown by the fact that they reveal how people actually wore their clothes. The *Tailor and Cutter* in 1877 published the comment that 'few gentlemen, even in summer, wear their coats open'. Yet the cartes very seldom show men with coat jackets

42 (opposite, top left). *Woven patterns, especially stripes of all kinds, were popular for Victorian fabrics. By 1870 summer dresses could be of silk or muslin. This young woman's dress is of muslin mounted on a cotton lining. It is trimmed with ruffles of the same material, cut on the cross and unlined. The stripes of the dress can be seen through the ruffles. The skirt is double; an unlined overskirt, open at the front and edged with a ruffle, is worn over a lined underskirt. The dress is finished with a lace collar fastened by a brooch. A cross on a wide ribbon is worn below the collar. The woman wears her hair in heavy coiled braids. Her jewellery includes drop ear-rings and a bracelet made of flat medallions linked together. The photographer, William Savage of Winchester, seems to have been one of the more imaginative in his use of 'props': this woman holds a frond of fern in her hand.*

43 (opposite, top right). *An old lady photographed in the early 1870s in a fashionable dress that has many echoes of the 1860s in it. The braid trimming at the top of her sleeves is the last vestige of the epaulettes of an earlier decade. So too is her puffed-out hairstyle. However, her hair does not hide her ears and she is wearing very elaborate ear-rings. The frilled sleeves and the double-apron overskirt are all part of 1870s fashion. Her cap is of crocheted lace trimmed with flat ribbon bows. She has a matching shoulder scarf and little collar.*

44 (opposite, bottom left). *The back of this carte bears the inscription 'In remembrance of Frida Euting, 6 Devon Square, Newton Abbot, February 26th 1875'. The carte was taken by W. Phelps of Newton Abbot and shows a woman wearing a very fashionable dress with a double skirt. The top is made as a princess-line tunic. She is in half-mourning, for her dress is trimmed with bands of crepe. Her hair is braided at the back, as well as being wound high on her head in a chignon. The inscription is a little ambiguous, for it could mean that the woman in the picture is in mourning for Frida, or it could mean that she is Frida herself and the photograph could have been sent to someone else by her family. In the latter case, the fact that she is in mourning is coincidental. The Victorians had many conventions about mourning clothes and many women and children wore black clothing for long periods.*

45 (opposite, bottom right). *A woman in a silk dress trimmed with velvet. The front of the bodice is plain velvet as are the cuffs and the ribbon banding on the back of the skirt. Two contrasting colours and fabrics such as this began to be fashionable in the 1870s and were to be carried to extremes in the 1880s. A great deal of jewellery was worn in the 1870s and as well as a brooch, a pendant on a short chain and a wide wedding ring this woman wears a chatelaine at her waist. This consists of a number of metal chains all fastened to a clasp or hook which is attached to a belt or the waistband of the dress. At the lower end of the chains were fastened needlework accessories, keys or other personal items.*

completely buttoned up. Waistcoats were always very firmly buttoned. (It was not until much later that Edward, Prince of Wales, left the bottom button on his waistcoat undone and set a fashion that was to last well into the twentieth century.) If a coat was done up it seems to have been fastened by the top button only, and this must have been the normal practice.

The top hat continued to be the basic wear of the middle classes, but a wide variety of hats was being introduced during the 1870s. These were very largely for sporting occasions and were to become more commonly worn over the next two decades. The artisans and labouring classes wore softer hats in rather shapeless styles, the most common being the 'billycock' hat.

1880 to 1890

As the 1880s progressed women's dresses gradually became plainer and more severe; the cartes show this change very well. The narrow, tie-back skirt was often replaced by a pleated skirt in the first two years of the decade, although the pleats were sometimes caught into place on a narrow lining, which had the effect of turning it into a narrow skirt. The princess line was still fashionable. Between 1881 and 1883 the bustle returned, this time much higher and larger in outline. Gone were the curves and

46 (opposite, top left). *A young woman, photographed in Southsea about 1874, wearing a flowing velvet dress lavishly trimmed with lace and braid. The back of the overskirt is draped up over a bustle. The underskirt is probably trained. The dress has a demure high neckline, softened by a small white collar, fastened by a brooch. Buttons covered with braid fasten the front of the bodice and decorate the sleeves. Her hair is wound round her head like a crown and her jewellery includes a star-shaped pendant.*

47 (opposite, top right). *An older woman in a dress made in stiffened silk decorated with velvet, lace and braid. Her hair is wound up into a braided crown, but in spite of its dangling ringlets (which may well be false) it is not luxuriant. She too wears a brooch at the neck, a pendant and a watch. The picture shows clearly how the watch is worn in a small pocket at her waist with its chain passed through a buttonhole; a decorated fob is attached to the free end of the chain. This woman is the mother (or possibly the grandmother) of the two girls in plate 31. Her name is also Burta and her picture was taken by J. Gilchrist of Edinburgh about 1875.*

48 (opposite, bottom left). *A studious, looking young woman with metal-rimmed spectacles whose carte is dated on the back as 1876. Her dress, with its double apron overskirt, is a little old-fashioned for this date, but her hairstyle, with the neat bun worn high on the crown of her head with a dangling ribbon, is high fashion, for by 1875-6 the masses of false hair were disappearing. The sleeve trimming is typical of the mid 1870s and her embroidered scarf is fastened by two brooches.*

49 (opposite, bottom right). *By the end of the 1870s a narrow princess-line style of dress was fashionable. The hairstyle had also become smoother and neater. The young woman's dress is made of two contrasting fabrics and is figure-fitting almost to her knees, where the skirt divides to show a ruched underskirt. Her watch pocket is a feature on the outside of her dress and she wears, in addition to drop ear-rings, a great collarette of dark beads, possibly jet, which cascade over her chest. Many dresses of the 1880s had in them an element of 'fancy-dress'. The carte was taken about 1878-9.*

50 (left). *A carte showing the five children of one family; the back of the carte is inscribed* 'Taken 1872 at Mr Webster's studio'. *There is no trade plate on the back of the carte. The eldest of the family is the young woman in a long, light-coloured dress having a skirt made with three flounces. The skirt is comparatively narrow and she probably wore no bustle under this summer seaside dress. Over the dress she wears a stiff, wide belt and a large cross on a dark ribbon. Her hair is held back in a long 'pony-tail' style and she is possibly eighteen years old. Her brother, behind her, is possibly sixteen years old and the picture does not show his clothes clearly. The two youngest girls, on either side, are dressed alike in dark dresses — navy serge was very popular for girls' seaside dresses — with frills on the bodices and also on the mid calf-length double skirt. They have narrow edgings of white at neck and cuffs. The younger of the two carries a bucket and spade. The other girl, on the right of the picture, probably about thirteen or fourteen years old, wears a calf-length dress trimmed with frills of the same material and picked out with a darker velvet ribbon.*

51 (right). *A husband and wife portrayed in 1870. The man wears dark trousers and a short frock coat with a velvet collar. His waistcoat and shirt are white, and worn with a dark-toned tie. By the 1870s a man who was not clean-shaven wore a moustache or a short full beard and moustache as in this picture. His seated wife wears a silk dress trimmed with velvet ribbon; the dress has a double skirt with the front of the overskirt open and turned back to give the effect of a jacket with long basques at the front. The back of the overskirt would be draped up over the bustle. She wears a patterned scarf tucked into the neckline of her dress. Under the dress bodice she wears a white chemisette. Her hairstyle is not as elaborate as*

those pictured on page 30, but the back hair is still braided across the crown of her head. Both husband and wife wear watches in little pockets on the left side of their torsos and both have watch chains draped to pass through a button hole in the centre front of their clothes.

52 (left). *For this carte William Savage of Winchester took the rustic stile from his studio into his garden where a father and daughter pose elegantly in early 1870s summer clothes. The man wears a white waistcoat, striped trousers and a bow tie under a frock coat. His straw hat is narrow-brimmed with a broad ribbon. The girl wears a white or pastel coloured dress with a frill round the hem and on the sleeves. Her bodice has a fluted peplum at the back, emphasising her bustle. Her little hat is straw with a silk crown trimmed with flowers. Because of her hairstyle, with its heavy braids, she must wear the hat tilted over her eyes. It is held in place by a ribbon passing under her braids at the back. She also has a ribbon round her neck tied in a flat bow at the back with long ends. One of these ends is brought forward over her shoulder and hangs down the front of her bodice.*

53 (right). *This carte has the inscription on the back 'Samuel Saltmarsh and his four sons, Charles Prior, Cecil, William & Samuel'. The smallest boy, at the back (presumably Samuel), is wearing a jacket trimmed with braid, but the other three are dressed alike in sailor suits, each complete with lanyard and a big patch pocket. Under the sailor jackets they are wearing shirts with bow ties; they have a second bow on their chests. Their trousers are cut off below the knee and with them they wear white stockings and ankle boots. The picture was taken in the late 1870s.*

54 (left). *Three-year-old Harry Canning posed for this carte-de-visite on 25th May 1877.*
Like all small boys of the time he wears a dress. Harry's dress is of tartan trimmed with lace
at the neck and with large buttons or wool pompoms on the skirt. The short sleeves of the
dress are tied up with ribbons to make them even shorter and this extends the neckline to give
an almost 'off-the-shoulder' effect. He also wears three-quarter length socks and neat ankle
boots.

55 (right). *This small boy was about four years old when he was photographed in 1871 and*
had been promoted out of dresses into a velvet knickerbocker suit lavishly trimmed with
braid. He wears striped socks and ankle boots and carries a Scottish bonnet. The clothes he
wears are typical of the mid 1860s and early 1870s, for the trousers are gathered at the knee.
During the 1870s this style went out of fashion and a boy's trousers were cut straight just
below the knee. The 'rustic' background is typical of the 1870s.

56 (opposite, left). *A little girl, probably no more than two years old, at the end of the*
1870s. Her smart princess-line coat is very obviously influenced by adult fashions and she
wears with it a scuttle-shaped hat, tied under her chin with a ribbon. Under the coat she has
on a light-coloured dress, white stockings and the ankle-strap shoes which were worn by
little children throughout the nineteenth century. Had she been a year older she would have
been wearing ankle boots. Ankle-strap shoes were a sign of babyhood, but girls would have
worn them for about a year longer than boys.

57 (opposite, right). *A seven-year-old girl in a double skirt, the overskirt caught up at the*
sides, and a jacket bodice. She may be in mourning for her jacket seems to be trimmed with
crepe and she has a crepe band on her round hat. Round her neck she has a chain carrying a
medallion or a watch. Her hair is held back by an 'Alice' band and she wears buttoned
boots.

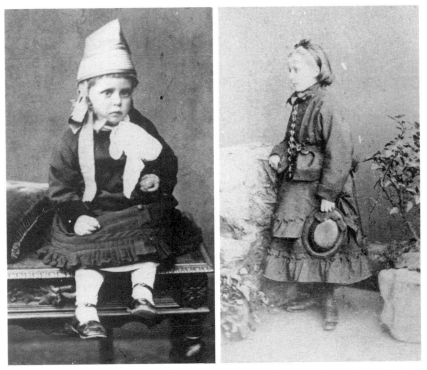

frills and fringing of the 1870s, both on skirts and bodices. Skirts of the 1880s were draped and swathed, but the fabrics were firmer and pleated edgings replaced the soft ruffles of the 1870s. Bodices in the 1880s fitted the figure and were buttoned up the front to the throat. Gone were the low necklines and the insertions and jabots. A small standing collar was the 1880s fashion, often edged with a small upstanding 'pie-crust' frill or a small ruff. The heavy hairstyles disappeared and heads became smooth again with a bun at the back. The most fashion-conscious wore a small fringe over the forehead, which was sometimes crimped into straggly waves or curls.

Although some small girls in the 1880s wore scaled-down versions of adult dress, their clothes were beginning to be more sensible and practical. Smocking was used across the yoke, at first as a novelty in the early 1880s, but later it became almost universal for children's clothes, a fashion which was combined with a broad soft sash round the hips below the waist. Princess-line dresses, with contrasting vertical panels in the front,

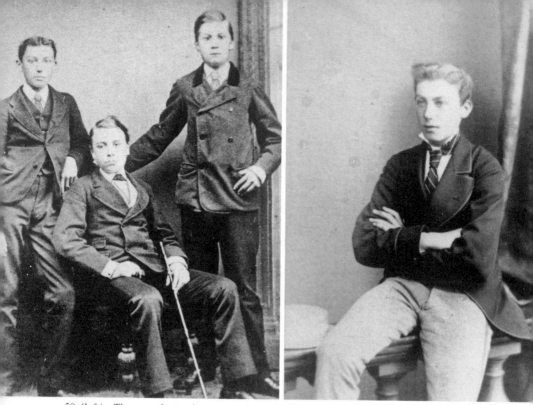

58 (left). *Three students photographed on 5th November 1870 at the Legord studio in Lewisham, Kent. Their names, which they signed at the bottom of the mount of the carte, are S. Shore, H. Fraze and D. Stillwell. S. Shore, at the left of the group, wears a single-breasted jacket over matching waistcoat and trousers. This is actually a lounge suit, although his jacket is shorter than usual. H. Fraze, seated, wears matching trousers and a double-breasted jacket with a light waistcoat. Note the little ticket pocket on the right-hand side of his jacket. D. Stillwell wears a 'reefer' type jacket, double-breasted, with a velvet collar, over slightly darker trousers. (This is unusual: for most of the nineteenth century men wore dark jackets over lighter-toned trousers.) Gradually these changed to matching clothes, but a jacket lighter toned than trousers is rare.)*

59 (right). *Another young man, photographed on 11th August 1871. He is very conventionally dressed in a morning coat and light trousers with a darker line down the outside seam. His diagonally striped tie is worn round a stand-up collar. On the balustrade beside him is a low-crowned straw hat. These had been worn in summer by young men since the 1850s. Until the 1860s they had ribbon ends dangling at the back. When women adopted this fashion in the early 1860s men abandoned it and wore their straw hats with plain ribbon bands and no streamers.*

60 (opposite, left). *A young man and an older man from a carte dated 1872. It was taken at Ballater, Scotland, and the men could be father and son. Both wear lounge suits; the older man's is made of tweed. The young man is holding a Glengarrie cap. These were fashionable in England for sporting occasions, such as playing croquet, or for walking in the country. In Scotland they were worn by schoolboys in town, and by adults when wearing a kilt, or with Norfolk jacket and knickerbockers out on the moors.*

61 (opposite, right). *A young man on his graduation day in the early 1870s. Like the young man in plate 59, he wears trousers with a darker stripe down the outer seam. The rest of his clothes are hidden by his graduate's gown but he probably wears a waistcoat and a morning coat over a shirt. His tie is knotted below a turn-down collar. His mortar board rests on the table beside him. The arm rest he is leaning on is a feature of many photographers' studios in the 1870s and 1880s. Often they were the elaborate backs of the studio chair padded to make a 'rest' as an aid to making a pose.*

were also worn by small girls, again with a broad sash round the hips. For older girls, from ten to fourteen years, a dress with a double skirt, the top of dark serge and the lower of striped cotton, and with the top skirt draped up at the back, was a fashionable craze. It was known as the 'Newhaven fishwife' dress and was similar to those pictured in the photographs taken by Hill and Adamson in the 1840s. The alternative to this style was a version of the sailor suit worn by boys, but with a pleated skirt and a hip sash instead of trousers. Jersey pullovers were worn by both girls and boys for seaside holidays or on casual occasions.

Small boys wore sailor suits or Norfolk jackets over short trousers cut off just below the knee. Another popular style for very small boys (popular with their mothers, although not, it would appear from recorded memories, with the boys themselves) was the 'Little Lord Fauntleroy' suit consisting of velvet trousers and jacket worn with a blouse with a spreading frilled collar. Other boys wore smaller versions of the adult lounge suit or the Norfolk jacket.

Men's clothes show more variety in the 1880s. There are few frock coats in 1880s cartes-de-visite, even among the elderly, normal wear being either a morning-coat suit or a lounge suit. Top hats, bowlers or straw hats could be worn with either of

62 (left). *Smocking, gathering and gauging were fashionable innovations at the end of the 1870s and the beginning of the 1880s, giving ease and fullness and achieving a softer effect than the pleating which was an alternative fashion. This young woman, photographed by W. Stevenson of Todmorden, Yorkshire, wears a princess-line dress with the new gauged sleeves of 1881. The dressmakers complained that, owing to the rows of gatherings on sleeves that made up the gauging, 'the work is doubled'. The fashion remained popular until the return of the bustle in 1883, when it largely disappeared from adult wear, although remaining in use on children's clothes. The skirt of this dress is swathed round the thighs where a frilled skirt is attached with more gauging. In spite of the large bows holding the horizontal pleats of the skirt in place, front and back (the edge of the back one can be seen below the left elbow), the dress and hairstyle give a plain, almost severe impression after the frills and cascading lace of a decade before.*

63 (centre). *A carte from Heath and Bullingham's studio in Plymouth showing how widespread was the use of the photographer's padded and decorated arm rest. These rests were often also the top of the back of the chair. This woman, photographed in 1882, is also wearing a princess-line dress, but made in contrasting wool and velvet fabrics. Her watch pocket is very evident, as is the chain and fob of her watch. The skirt of her dress is draped in horizontal folds caught up in front and at the back. She wears a dark lace collar over her dress with a white edging just visible above it; this white edging is a small 'pie-crust' frill. She also wears ear-rings and a wide wedding ring.*

64. *Lizzie Smith, wife of Jim Smith, was photographed by E. Birchley of Birmingham about 1886. She wears a short cut-velvet cape over a bodice (the sleeves of which have long close-fitting cuffs), and a double skirt. The underskirt is pleated in narrow folds which are probably caught together at the back of the fabric to make the skirt narrow and flat in front. (This 'catching' shows at the bottom, where the lower part of the skirt is left free as an aid to walking.) The overskirt is open in front and is draped up over a bustle pad at the back. Her hat is a toque made of gauged fabric, probably silk, decorated with a white feather trim at one side. Her short, dark curly fringe shows beneath it.*

65. *The Searle Brothers opened their studio at 191 Brompton Road in south-west London in 1882. One of their cartes shows this young middle-class couple in a typical Victorian 'husband and wife' pose. The young woman, with softly fringed hair, wears a box-pleated skirt below a tartan overskirt and a very tight jacket. This jacket and overskirt have their lower edges cut into tabs, reminiscent of mid seventeenth-century fashions. The front-opening overskirt is draped and folded over the bustle at the back. This style can be dated to the mid 1880s. The young man wears a morning coat. (The seam just below the waist which distinguishes this from a lounge jacket is clearly visible.) He wears it firmly buttoned up in the way advocated by the 'Tailor and Cutter' in the late 1870s, and he may be considered rather old-fashioned for, by 1886, 'the Gentlemans Magazine of Fashion' advocated the wearing of morning coats unbuttoned or done up by only one button.*

66 (opposite, top left). *The most important fashion innovation in the 1880s was the rise of the tailor-made suit. Close-fitting plain clothes, based on men's fashions, had long been worn by women for riding, but the new sports and activities that became available to women and the greater freedom that these brought led to the adoption of a 'riding-habit' type of clothes for everyday wear. A plain skirt and neatly fitting jacket, like that shown here on a carte from H. P. Robinson's studio in Tunbridge Wells, would be suitable for walking or golfing or even (after the invention of the safety bicycle, with two equal-sized wheels, in 1885) for cycling. Tailoring was also used for women's and girls' coats in the 1880s. This plain skirt, over a small bustle, with a neat double-breasted jacket, worn with a plain round hat with a feather trim, is typical of early 1880s tailoring. The woman also wears a short curly fringe, above-the-wrist gloves and carries the stout-handled umbrella of the period.*

67 (opposite, top right). *Tailoring became fashionable for indoor clothes as well as outdoor; this woman wears a tailored jacket made in cut-velvet (patterned velvet was a feature of 1880s fashions). The severity of the style is softened by the beauty of the fabric itself and by the lace at neck and wrists. Note the elegance shown by the placing of the brooch at the neck, set to one side instead of the centre. This carte shows well the slightly tousled curly fringe of hair of the early 1880s.*

68 (opposite, bottom left). *A young woman in mourning. Her dress has a knee-high band of crepe around the hem and a panel of crepe down the front. Her sleeves are covered with crepe from wrist to elbow. This would be the first stage of mourning, which, for a husband, would be worn for a year and a day; after this she would go into half-mourning for nine months, lessening the amount of crepe on her clothes. Finally the third stage of mourning, for a further three months, omitted the crepe and permitted plain black and white, before returning to colours. The necklace, brooch and ear-rings she is wearing would be of carved jet. By the mid 1880s the bustle had returned and the fringe was disappearing. This dress, though plainly cut, showing the influence of the tailoring, has an obviously full skirt, achieved by goring rather than gathering, which would be drawn up by the bustle at the back. Note the photographer's 'rest', here obviously the back of the chair.*

69 (opposite, bottom right). *By the end of the 1880s many women were allowing their fringes to grow, brushing the hair back loosely from the face. Sometimes this was done over a small pad of false hair, to give a fuller frame to the face. The back hair was still confined in a bun. The dress of this woman from Sheffield shows the transition of fashion from the 1880s to the 1890s. Her skirt is loosely draped up to her bustle, but her bodice has the sleeves set in with a pleat at the top, heralding the style of sleeves of the 1890s. These sleeves have silk cuffs with a frill of dark lace falling over the hand and she wears the typical 'pie-crust' frill of white of the 1880s at her neck.*

these. Sporting costume and casual clothes were becoming popular, from the knee breeches and patrol jackets worn by the keen cyclist to the white trousers and striped blazers worn for tennis and boating. Norfolk jackets were country casual wear and a variety of pillbox hats, caps and straw hats were worn with the sporting clothes appropriate to the occasion.

1890 to 1900

By the 1890s the carte-de-visite was beginning to come to the end of its popularity. The larger cabinet print, introduced in 1866, had become in a little over two decades the normal size for a studio portrait. The cartes-de-visite of the 1890s were the cheaper end of the market. Fashion, however, like photography, was within the reach of all but a very few and there is little difference

70 (left). *A very small boy photographed by G. West and Son of Southsea in 1883 or 1884. He wears a white dress, lavishly covered in white eyelet embroidery, over embroidered white drawers. The skirt of the dress is made in two flounces and it has an embroidered yoke, like a baby's bib. The fashion touch that marks this dress out as the 1880s is the wide sash worn round the hips. This is slotted through two loops, made of the fabric of the dress, to keep it in place. He wears the ankle-strap shoes of babyhood and is probably about two years old. The toy he is carrying is a pop-gun, with its cork fastened to the body of the gun by a string.*

71 (right). *Another toddler, possibly a year older, this little girl wears a smocked and tucked dress in a style that was to be fashionable for almost two decades, although the 1890s would remove the low sash and leave the dress hanging free from its yoke. She too wears the ankle-strap shoes of a baby. Her bonnet, however, is not a baby's bonnet but the rural sun-bonnet which would have been worn by country girls up to and into womanhood. The middle classes used them only for little girls' wear.*

72 (opposite, left). *Mother and daughter in the clothes of the early 1880s. Although the curly fringe was fashionable it was not adopted by all women. This woman's hairstyle is uncompromisingly severe, but her dress is fashionable. The girl's dress is similar but has a knee-length skirt worn over black stockings. She wears an adult-like frill of white at her neck. These were tacked inside the neckband of the dresses and could be easily removed for washing and replaced by fresh ones. Note the basket of flowers. This was another 'prop' of the 1880s photographer's studio, often used in pictures of young girls.*

73 (opposite, right). *A small boy about four years old, in the mid 1880s, wearing a serge sailor suit. His bloused bodice is worn over very short trousers which would just have covered his knees when he stood up. Lace-up shoes began to replace ankle boots for children during the late 1880s and were very much more comfortable to wear.*

in the clothes shown in the studio cartes between the dress of town and country women, rich and poor, save perhaps the occasions on which they would wear them.

The last decade of the nineteenth century showed further changes in fashion, and the use of tailor-made suits for women. Daytime skirts were plain, drapery and ornamentation disappearing with the bustle. These plain skirts were fitted at the waist, smooth over the hips, and any fullness was taken to the back. The skirts were not narrow; they were usually made of several panels and were easy to wear compared with the constraints of the previous twenty years. All the fashion emphasis was on the top half of the body.

Dress bodices, and the blouses worn beneath the tailored jackets, could be very elaborate. As if to emphasise this, many of the 1890s cartes-de-visite are head and shoulders only — a new style of popular photography — or, at the most, three-quarter length. These portraits show women with their hair taken back to a bun, without fringes, and wearing very high-necked dresses

74 (left). *A boy, aged about nine or ten years, in a corduroy velvet jacket and trousers, worn with a tweed waistcoat and a deerstalker hat. He also wears a very adult wing collar, although his tie is hidden by the jacket, which buttons high on the chest, a feature of men's jackets of all kinds in the 1880s. Although he is young, similar clothes would have been worn by countrymen of all ages from the 1840s onward. This countryman's suit was the inspiration for the lounge suit of the upper and middle classes. This boy looks as if his suit is new, or at least his best one. He could be attending a wedding for he wears a spray of flowers in his top buttonhole.*

75 (right). *A middle-aged man in a single-breasted reefer jacket worn with tweed trousers. His clothes, and his style of facial hair, could have been worn at any time from the 1860s but the bowler hat he holds is very much of the 1880s. The first bowler hats appeared in the 1860s and were 'pudding basin' shaped — sometimes even flat on top — and had very narrow rims. In the 1870s they had very high crowns and in the 1880s and 1890s they became the bowlers that are still worn a century later, with a medium crown and a brim well curled up at the sides. Note the balustrade, with a country backcloth, which came back into favour in photographers' studios in the 1880s.*

76 (opposite). *The 'safety' bicycle, with two equal-sized wheels, was invented in 1885 and a great many variations on this theme were made in the following ten years. The bicycle in this outdoor carte, taken by H. Bates of Hampton, Middlesex, can be dated to between 1888 and 1890. It has solid tyres and a fixed wheel. (Note the foot rests on the front forks, for use while going down hill when one did not need to pedal.) The machine is either a 'Referee' or a 'Wulfruna' for both had the same shape frame with slightly sloping cross-bar. The proud owner of the bicycle wears a lounge suit and the flat cap that was fashionable for country wear and outdoor pastimes. To save his trouser ends catching in the spokes he wears gaiters, made like a countryman's leather gaiters, but in cloth for ease of movement. They fasten with three straps and buckles.*

77 (top). *In the 1890s the format of some of the cartes-de-visite changed and a variety of studio 'gimmicks' was employed. This 1896 multiple portrait of Miss Ethel Brownrigg-Jay, a well known society beauty, shows her posed in front of a triple bamboo-framed mirror. The carte is turned on its side to accommodate this effect. For fashion historians such cartes are most useful for they show the back, front and side of the hairstyle in which the front hair is combed back over a pad of false hair and gathered into a loose chignon at the back of the head. The dress is of pleated dark silk with a double frill collar. The neck is low enough to reveal a simple chain necklace. Dresses with this neckline, with or without sleeves, are seen*

with stand-up collars. In the first half of the decade their sleeves gradually became wider at the shoulder — the leg of mutton sleeve — and by 1895 are sometimes a double sleeve, the top half being a huge puffed short sleeve, with a narrow long sleeve worn below it. In 1897 the wide sleeve suddenly ceased to be fashionable, and long, close-fitting sleeves were worn instead. The dress bodices, often cut and draped to look like a jacket, or with a contrasting front panel, were tucked, folded and draped as elaborately as the skirts of the previous two decades. Blouses were usually a lighter colour and fabric than the skirts and jackets and could be as full and frilly as the wearer wished. Lace or lace trimmings were very popular, as were white lawn or cotton, with whitework embroidery. Tucks, both vertical and horizontal, were a fashionable form of decoration.

White cotton with a great deal of white embroidery was the almost universal wear for babies and toddlers, all of whom appear in the cartes very elaborately dressed in a great many layers of clothing. Children are the only people who appear full-length in the 1890s cartes. Over the befrilled and tucked dresses they wore pinafores, some of which were almost as decorative as the dress beneath.

Little girls and young boys are shown in sombre-coloured clothes echoing the adult styles. Some little girls seem to have worn hats, collars and sleeves as large as those worn by adult women, only the shorter skirts being a concession to childhood. Small boys seem to have suffered the same fate. The top half of their clothing had a similar style to that worn by adult men, but with short trousers and long stockings covering the knees.

Men's clothes remained very much in the same fashions and styles as in the 1880s, although they seem to be a little baggier and more crumpled. The morning-coat suit was normal middle-class and professional wear, while a variety of reefer jackets was worn by working men. The lounge suit was, however, rapidly gaining favour among all social classes, and as such was a great fashion

in the photographs of many actresses or society beauties published in magazines such as 'The Strand Magazine' of the 1890s. For daytime wear the normal neckline was very high although for younger women and girls it could be a little lower. This carte was taken by Miller Studios of Great Yarmouth.

78 (bottom). The back of another 1890s carte-de-visite, this time by R. Hammond of Bacup, Lancashire. The designs on the backs of the cartes were also turned on their sides. The 'classical' robes of the female figure are very much in the style of the aesthetic dress of the period as is the setting in which she appears. Photographers of the 1890s stressed the fact that they were artists. Many provincial studios sold artists' materials — papers, paints and canvasses — and made picture frames as part of their normal business; their advertisements in the local 'town guides' carried this information.

leveller. An observer at Charing Cross station, London, in 1897 reported: 'There were nearly two lounges to one morning coat and quite three lounges to one frock coat.' This possibly represents the proportions of the social classes (or ages) of the men using the station as much as a pure fashion trend, but it is nevertheless significant. Frock coats do not seem to feature in the cartes-de-visite of the 1890s, while the morning coat and the lounge suit are both quite common, with a greater proportion of men in the lounge suit.

79 (opposite, top left). *A common form of carte-de-visite in the 1890s was the head and shoulders portrait. As the skirts of the 1890s were very plain, with all the decorations concentrated on the upper part of the body, these portraits still tell us much about the fashions of the decade. This girl wears a wool, or wool and cotton fabric, dress decorated with strip panels of clustered small beads. Such beaded panels were popular in the 1890s but, by the standards of the day, this would have been considered a very plain dress. The high standing collar, with its 'pie-crust' frill, was fashionable in the 1880s and continued in popularity into the 1890s. The collar is fastened with a small brooch. The sleeves of the dress are pleated into the armhole to give the 'kick-up' effect that dates the carte to the early years of the decade. Note the girl's simple metal-rimmed spectacles. Their design has not changed at all from those worn in the 1870s or 1880s (see plates 3 and 48). This carte was taken at Horsham, West Sussex.*

80 (opposite, top right). *A young woman wearing an afternoon dress of about 1895. It is made of striped silk with plain silk sleeves and front panel. The bodice of this dress is gauged, and trimmed with a braid made of small beads set as a floral pattern. The narrower braid round her collar has a velvet ribbon threaded through it. She, too, has a 'pie-crust' frill edging the top of her collar. Her sleeves show how the fashions developed, for by 1895 sleeves had huge puffs to the upper arm (see plate 15).*

81 (opposite, bottom left). *The tailored suit that had become an alternative to a dress in the 1880s became even more popular in the 1890s. Although close-fitting and practical it still followed fashion, the sleeves in particular rising, expanding and then contracting again during the decade. Under the suit jacket a blouse was worn. This was usually made of cotton or linen and could be quite masculine in cut, even having a stiffened collar and tie. This girl wears a lace jabot and white collar with her striped blouse and tailored suit, whose sleeves place it about 1896.*

82 (opposite, bottom right). *From 1897 to the end of the nineteenth century sleeves became steadily closer fitting. The bodice fronts of dresses became even more elaborate, and contrasting panels, tucked and frilled, became common. Differing fabrics were mixed together in the same dress in bewildering variety. The hairstyles of the 1890s could be widely differing. Some young women favoured a curly fringe as in the early 1880s, while others took their hair straight back from the forehead, sometimes over pads. The bun at the back was usually large and loose, or padded out with false hair. Partings were uncommon.*

83 (left). *A woman in a dark dress showing the first of the fantastic sleeve styles of the 1890s. At the beginning of the decade sleeves were pleated into the armhole at the top to produce the 'kick-up' sleeve that gradually became larger and developed into the 'leg-of-mutton' sleeve. In 1891 these sleeves were still fairly narrow. This is a two-piece dress, almost like a tailored suit, although the dark panel between the revers is more likely to be an integral part of the bodice rather than a separate blouse. Many dress bodices of the 1890s looked like jackets over blouses but were actually made all in one with detachable cuffs and neck frills. Skirts were nearly always simple, smooth over the hips and with any fullness drawn to the back in a pleat at the centre. The plain white fan shown here may well be a photographer's 'prop' rather than an accessory owned by this woman. In the 1890s fans were used in the evenings but not often in the day; they were usually made of ostrich feathers.*

84 (right). *In the middle of the 1890s the tops of sleeves became very much enlarged and were often made in two parts with a short, very puffed sleeve worn over a long close-fitting undersleeve. In 1896 and 1897 a limp version of this style became fashionable as shown in this picture. Instead of being pleated or gathered at the shoulder, which created the puffed effect, the sleeves were set in smoothly but then became very large and were gathered at the elbow into a long tight cuff covering the forearm. This girl's dress bodice has an inserted plastron front, slightly pouched at the waist, of a contrasting colour. It is set between two vertical frills of the dress fabric and there is a frill of the inserted fabric at the neck of the dress. This dress is influenced by the 'aesthetic' movement and has a low neckband shaped to a gentle vee-shape at the front rather than the customary stand-up collar. Below a very tightly swathed waistband, with a large steel-cut buckle, the skirt is plain and straight. The wearer is probably in her mid-teens and her back hair hangs loose. The front hair is taken back from her forehead in a soft roll and is held in place by decorative combs or a clasp. Compare this dress with the 'classical' robes depicted on the back of an 1890s carte in plate 78.*

85 (top left). *A dark-haired baby from Horsham, Sussex, wearing a white dress, the sleeves embroidered with white eyelet embroidery. Over the dress he or she, for there was no difference in babies' clothing, wears a plain cotton pinafore, the shoulders of which are tied up with ribbons in the way that small children's dresses were a generation before. The pinafore, which is really an overall, fastens at the neck at the back. Ankle-strap shoes and white socks complete the picture.* 86 (top right). *A second baby, this time from Bacup, Lancashire, wears more elaborate clothes. The dress would appear, from this carte taken by Oakley and Sidebottom, to be coloured and there is a lavishly embroidered white pinafore on top. The dress has large puffed sleeves, echoing adult fashions, and two tucks round the hem. The pinafore has an extra frill at the neck. The embroidered cotton from which it is made is machine embroidered and could be purchased by the yard to be made up into babies' or children's clothes.* 87 (left). *Florence Dora Wills was photographed, at the age of sixteen months, at Christmas, 1900. She stands on a staircase (which may simply be a few stairs in the photographer's studio) in her long-sleeved white dress with tucks round the hem. Her ankle-strap shoes with bows on the front are similar to those worn by little Princess Maud in the 1870s. The skirt of her dress hangs from a vertically tucked yoke which is edged with a*

small frill. The sleeves are large and wide, gathered into a cuff at the wrists. Although this carte was taken at the end of the century, small boys and girls would have worn clothes like this all through the 1890s, normally with a pinafore over the dress.

88 (right). Photographed by Mora Studios of Brighton, this little girl of the mid 1890s wears a hat and coat that are a miniature version of the fashionable adult world. Her big square collar is edged with either a fine thick fur or plush, as is the band of her matching 'tam-o-shanter' hat. Note the buckle in the hat band. It was probably cut steel, but could have been set with marquisite or glass 'stones'.

89 (opposite, top left). A twelve or thirteen-year-old schoolboy of the 1890s in a short Eton jacket (nicknamed the 'bum-freezer' jacket). With this short jacket he wears high-waisted long trousers and a waistcoat, the lapels of which follow the shape of those on his jacket. His shirt has a deep turn-down collar. Both this style of jacket and of collar were known as 'Eton' in spite of the fact that boys from many schools all over Britain wore them over a period of almost eighty years. The traditional rivalry between Eton and Harrow schools resulted in Eton boys wearing their collars inside their jackets and Harrow boys wearing them turned over outside the jacket collar. This boy's school, in Sunderland, obviously followed the fashion set by Harrow School. His hat is a round bowler.

90 (opposite, top right). A young man, wearing an early 1890s jacket of the style known as a 'lounge morning coat' because it had rounded cut-away lower fronts like a morning coat, but was made without a seam at the waist, like a lounge jacket. These jackets had five pockets, including an inside right breast pocket and a little ticket pocket above the right-hand outside pocket. This is clearly visible in the picture. Three of the four outside pockets normally had flaps over them, but the top left breast pocket did not; it was used to hold a handkerchief, the edge of which was left showing above the pocket. This man has a waistcoat to match his jacket and lighter-coloured tweed trousers. His shirt has a turn-down collar and his tie is a narrow 'four-in-hand'. He has a watch chain with a large fob and poses very elegantly with a smooth-finished walking cane.

91 (opposite, bottom left). Another teenage boy in the sports clothes of the 1890s, wearing white flannel trousers, white shirt and a striped blazer. By the middle of the decade it was permissible to leave off the waistcoat for sporting activities. It could be replaced with a wide cummerbund, but boys and very young men wore a wide canvas belt. Note the 'snake' buckle which was to continue into the twentieth century as part of every boy's apparel. The short knotted tie is also sports wear. The most significant fashion shown in this carte is the straw hat, symbol of the 1890s. It transcended class and was worn by men and women alike. This one is fastened to his lapel by a string.

92 (previous page, bottom right). *Sports clothes of the 1890s, showing just how much of men's wear had been adopted by women. This young woman's tailored suit has a velvet collar, fashionable for men since the 1860s. She also wears a stiffened collar, a tie and a straw hat; her hat band is narrower than that worn by the boy in plate 91, but it is fashion, not sex, that determines the width. By the end of the century all straw hat bands were narrow and often of two or more colours. This one has two colours in it, the darker at the top. Her shoes are pointed and laced, like a man's fashionable walking shoe. Only the skirt, plain and straight in front, gored and pleated at the back, is an essentially female garment. Her companion wears a soft flat cap, acceptable sports wear for gentlemen in the country. He also wears a bow tie and a soft collar to his shirt, the cuffs of which show below the sleeves of his lounge jacket. This carte, taken on the beach at Llandudno, shows two fashionably elegant young people in correct holiday attire.*

93 (below). *A photograph frame and albums for cartes-de-visite. The two photographs in the outer wings of the silver photograph frame were taken in the 1860s. The young woman in the centre is wearing the clothes of the 1870s. The small album dates from the 1860s, while the larger album was new in the 1880s.*

3. The Victorians as collectors

The family album

Every Victorian family in the second half of the nineteenth century had its photograph album. The usual type was a hard-backed book with leather covers, often embossed or gilded, with brass clasps to hold it together when shut. Inside, the pages were of stiff card, covered with paper. Holes were cut in the card so that the photographs sat in them, while the paper covers to the card had slightly smaller holes, so that the edges of the paper held the photographs in place. (All Victorian portraits were supplied to the public mounted on thin card. Two of these mounts, back to back, made up the thickness of the card pages of the albums.) The pages of the early 1860s albums had spaces cut to fit cartes-de-visite only, but from 1866 the albums were usually a mixture of cabinet-print sized spaces and carte-sized spaces arranged on alternate pages of the albums. Often the pages surrounding the spaces for the photographs were decorated with drawings or even colour pictures of sports, flowers or landscapes. Where the covers of the albums were not of leather, they could be of mother-of-pearl or even polished or lacquered wood. Some albums had musical boxes fitted in the back cover that played when the album was opened.

These albums became prized family possessions and many that survive today hold the photographs of three or even four generations of the same family. The best documented of these albums are still in the hands of the families whose portraits they hold, but some have found their way into museum collections. If the photographs in these old albums, at whatever social level, are named and dated, they become priceless historical treasures.

The fascination of old family albums lies in the fact that they reveal the Victorians as people who were known and loved by their families. Many of the 1890s photographs show people who were known to younger members of the same family still alive today. The pictures show the older generation at an earlier stage of life than their living relatives could have known them, so that a modern grandmother's crusty old uncle is, in the photograph album, an eager youth with his first bicycle, or a woman remembered as very elderly and frail is shown to have been a real beauty as a young woman. Family resemblances can also be found, as well as the knowledge of what our immediate ancestors wore. History learnt through such photographs becomes very real to the adult and child alike.

94. *A page from a carte-de-visite album with decorated pages. Embossed on the cover is the inscription 'J F M. October 26th 1878'. The theme of the decorations inside is of sports and pastimes; this page shows archery practice. The woman in the carte on the left is wearing a hat similar to that drawn at the top of the page, although her clothes are more those of 1875 than of 1878. The man on the right is wearing a tweed lounge suit and a bow tie. His clothes would have been fashionable from 1875 to 1885.*

95 (left). *Georgina Rummage, photographed at the Hay Studios, 68 Princes Street, Edinburgh, about 1870. She wears a dress with a double skirt, the upper one being longer in front (and probably the back) than at the sides. The bodice has a high neckline with a little frilled white collar, but gives the impression of the very fashionable low square neckline by the velvet and self-fabric folded trim around the buttoned insert across the chest. The sleeve ends are trimmed with velvet ribbon and are slit to reveal white frills. The two skirts are decorated with the same velvet ribbon. On the underskirt the ribbon alternates with wide tucks. Georgina wears her hair piled high in front and has long ringlets hanging down the back.*

96 (right). *Georgina's younger sister, Mary, wears an identical dress but without a bow at the neck; her collar is plain, not frilled. Both sisters wear little brooches at the neck and have a locket hanging from a chain. It was customary in Victorian times to dress sisters alike and both pictures were probably taken on the same occasion of a family visit to the photographer's studio. The album these cartes came from belonged to a Miss Moffat. All the people in the album are named and are probably related to each other. Most of the cartes were taken in various studios in Edinburgh between 1865 and 1885. There is one double page of cartes taken in America but the subjects have the same surnames as others in the book taken in Scottish studios. The album also contains two cartes of famous people, Princess Louise and Dugald Braidwood, were obviously collected by Miss Moffat.*

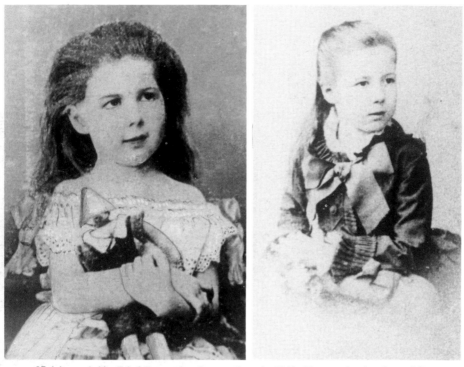

97 (above, left). *Ethel Brownrigg-Jay was born in 1869. She was the daughter of George Harvey Jay and Caroline Matilda Brownrigg. This carte is from the Brownrigg-Jay family album and shows the two year old Ethel wearing an embroidered white dress with the sleeves tied up with wide ribbons. (It is very similar to that worn by little Princess Maud in plate 110.) This carte is hand-coloured and Ethel's ribbons are blue. The clown doll and the striped silk scarf she is holding may well be photographer's 'props', for another carte from the album, obviously taken on the same occasion, shows Ethel and her older sister and brother, Grace and Harvey, in a group with the same doll and scarf and a rather battered wooden horse. These toys are far below the quality which one would expect of a family that had the aristocratic connections of the Brownrigg-Jays.*

98 (above, right). *Another carte of Ethel Brownrigg-Jay, dated 1876. She is seven years old and wears a dark-toned dress decorated with pleated frills and wide ribbons. Her high forehead and long hair were always considered beautiful by her family and here she wears her hair taken back and caught up at the back where it hangs down in a long pony-tail.*

99 (opposite, left). *Caroline Brownrigg-Jay, Ethel's mother. Ethel was Caroline's fifth and youngest child. In this mid 1870s carte Caroline wears a velvet dress with a low square neckline, lavishly trimmed with lace. The front of the skirt is open to reveal a gauzy underdress made in tiers of frills banded with ribbon. The neckline of her dress is filled in with three strands of large beads, and above these she wears a locket on a velvet ribbon. Her hair is piled high in a plaited crown and she has large floral pendant ear-rings. The basket of flowers is probably a photographer's 'prop'.*

100 (below, right). *Ethel Brownrigg-Jay, aged nine years, photographed in 1878 by C. Hawkins of Brighton. He also had a studio in Bath. Here Ethel wears a light-coloured summer dress with a white pinafore, buttoning on the shoulders, over the top. The frills round the armholes of her pinafore are worked in eyelet embroidery. She carries a straw hat which is trimmed with flowers and lined with a bright silk. Her hair is still held back in a pony-tail. Another carte of Ethel, as a young society beauty, appears in plate 77.*

101 (opposite, top left). *Young George Goldsmith, the son of George and Ellen Goldsmith of Hastings, Sussex, photographed by Henry Knight in the 1870s. He wears a sailor suit with short trousers and long dark stockings. The sides of the trousers have three lines of braid down them; the same braid decorates his wide collar and his pocket and cuffs. He wears a broad-brimmed straw hat, with the brim rolled upwards. This style of hat is known as a 'sailor's straw'. George Goldsmith grew up to become a soldier in the East Sussex Regiment, serving during the Boer War. Later he married and had children of his own.*

102 (opposite, top right). *Ellen Goldsmith, George's mother, photographed in the 1880s. By the time this picture was taken Ellen was a widow, her husband George having died in 1876, leaving her with two daughters, Alice and Annie, and George (left). Ellen was the daughter of a farmer near Rye, Sussex, and she and George Goldsmith married in 1851. They lived all their married life in Hastings, where their children were born. The two daughters both went into service before marrying tradesmen. At the time of his death George Goldsmith was running a public house in Hastings. Ellen may be wearing black, as did most widows in Queen Victoria's reign, but she is not in deep mourning. Her bodice is made of a plain fabric trimmed with velvet at neck and wrists, while her skirt, with its apron front and draped back, has a squared 'spot' pattern woven into it. This apron front and the 'tails' of the bodice are edged with jet beads. The buttons on her bodice are also of jet and she has a black, probably jet, and gold brooch at her throat. She wears a small white 'pie-crust' frill at her neck and her hair is neatly drawn back.*

103 (opposite, bottom left). *Edith Long, the grand-daughter of Ellen (above, right) and niece of George (above). Edith was the child of Ellen's second daughter, Annie. Edith was born in 1888 and this picture shows her at three years old. She wears a princess-line dress, of the kind that was fashionable for little girls from the end of the 1870s onward (see plate 56). The silver locket she is wearing belonged to her Aunt Alice, Ellen's elder daughter. It is still in the family and it, and the album of photographs, belong to a descendant of George and Ellen Goldsmith who still lives in Hastings. This picture of Edith and that of her grandmother were taken by J. W. Thomas of Hastings.*

104 (opposite, below right). *The back of the carte showing young George Goldsmith (above left). Henry Knight set up his studio in Grand Parade, St Leonards-on-Sea — just along the front from Hastings — in 1869-70. He is described in the 1871 census as a 'photographic artist' aged twenty-three years. Grand Parade was a very fashionable part of St Leonards and Henry Knight was a reputable photographer, gaining royal patronage. His studio contained several 'sets', one of which was the boat in which George Goldsmith was photographed; this was very popular with children. The last entry for Henry Knight in the local St Leonards directories is 1889.*

The cult of the celebrity

We can learn, too, what and who the Victorians were interested in. Not only were pictures of their own families popular with and collected by them, but the cartes-de-visite of the famous personalities of each decade were also added to the family albums. In an age when newspaper photography did not exist, commercially produced cartes enabled people to recognise the celebrities of their own time and to copy their clothes or style of wearing them. Many a now unnamed beauty adds a touch of theatrical glamour to the family album.

Many Victorian reporters commented on the crowds who flocked to see the new cartes of the famous in local photographers' windows. These cartes were produced commercially for resale by the bigger studios, A. and G. Taylor, Elliot and Fry, and Downey being among the leading London and provincial

105 (above, left). *David Rees, of 298 Clapham Road, London, photographed this man in the late 1870s. His name was William and he was reputed by his family to be a most handsome man. Later photographs of him show that he never lost his good looks. Here he wears a conventional morning suit, a turn-down collar and a 'four-in-hand' tie. A cabinet print from the same album taken in the 1880s shows him in knee breeches and patrol jacket with his large wheeled 'ordinary' (penny-farthing) bicycle.*

106 (above, right). *William's young wife, Martha, was photographed in the early 1880s. She wears a close-fitting jacket with a wide band of contrasting fabric round the hips. Her skirt was probably fairly narrow and may or may not have had a bustle. The sleeves of her jacket have deep cuffs of the same material as the hipband. Her hair has the soft curly fringe of the 1880s and she wears pendant floral ear-rings, a brooch at the neck and a locket on a velvet ribbon. The carte from the album was tinted and she has red lips, pink cheeks and blue eyes. By the time this carte was taken the studios were run by 'Rees Brothers and Son'.*

107 (opposite, left). *William and Martha's daughter was photographed by Hellis and Sons, in the mid 1880s. She wears an embroidered white dress with a wide sash tied in a big bow at the back. Her sleeves are elbow length and end in a little frill of eyelet embroidery. Similar clothes would have been worn by small children of either sex in the 1880s.*

108 (opposite, right). *The same photographer took another carte of the same girl in 1890. Here she wears a dress with a short pleated skirt. The bodice is hip-length and has a slightly shorter panel of velvet set in the front so that it looks like a jacket. Her short sleeves are gauged, or smocked, and then frilled at the elbow. She has a string of beads, probably coral, round her neck. The embroidered hem of her petticoat shows beneath her dress above black stockings and lace-up shoes. The basket of flowers is a photographer's 'prop'. The Japanese screen was one of the new backgrounds that came into fashion in the late 1880s.*

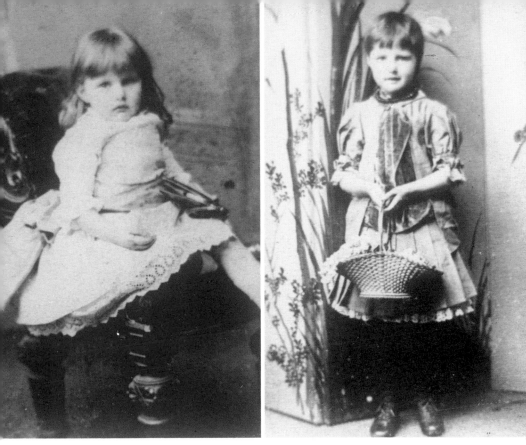

producers. The descendants of John Mayall uphold that, as photographers to the Royal Family, his studio never photographed actresses or published their pictures, but many other leading studios had no such scruples. The London Stercoscopic and Photographic Company regularly photographed society, sporting, theatrical, political and clerical people of note with the object of selling hundreds of copies of their portraits as cartes-de-visite. Both actresses and bishops were popular subjects but the greatest demand by far was for portraits of the Royal Family. The *Photographic Journal* of 15th February 1862 carried an article about cartes-de-visite of the famous in which the author said: 'Her Majesty's portraits, which Mr Mayall alone has taken, sell by the hundred thousand. No greater tribute to the memory of his Highness, the late Prince Consort, could have been paid than the fact that, within one week from his decease, no less than seventy thousand of his carte-de-visite were ordered from the house of Marion and Company in Regent Street.'

Marion and Company were photographic wholesalers who held stocks of thousands of different cartes waiting to be sent out to

109 (left). *His Royal Highness, Prince Arthur, Duke of Connaught and Strathern, Queen Victoria's third son and seventh child, was born in 1850 and had a distinguished military career from the early 1870s onward. Among other positions he was the Colonel of the Scots Guards and was often pictured in Scottish clothes. Here he wears Highland dress of kilt and Montrose jacket, both made in the same bold tartan. The jacket has more in common with the eighteenth century than with nineteenth-century clothes and he wears lace at his throat and wrists. He is also wearing false hair, added curls at the side of his head and an extra tail of hair, tied in a bag with a large bow at the back of the neck. Although taken in the 1870s or even 1880s these clothes and hairstyle would not have been out of place a hundred years before. Prince Arthur was a talented and romantic figure who, in 1879, married Princess Louise Marguerite of Prussia. Their children were Prince Arthur (1883-1938), Princess Margaret, who became the wife of Gustav VI of Sweden, and Princess, the Lady Patricia Ramsey. He became a field marshal in 1902 and from 1911 to 1916 was Governor General of Canada. He died in 1942.*

110 (right). *Her Royal Highness, Alexandra, Princess of Wales, the daughter of the King of Denmark, photographed in August 1872 with her youngest daughter, Princess Maud. From the time of her wedding to the Prince of Wales in 1863 Alexandra was one of the most popular of the Royal Family and her clothes, hairstyle and manners were widely copied. The Princess was photographed by many studios and thousands of cartes picturing her at all stages of her life, with or without her children, were bought by the Victorian public. This carte shows a simple dress, flat in front and curving over the bustle at the back, with pleated frills on the sleeves and round the edge of the front opening. Under it she would have worn*

another simple dress which would show in the front. In keeping with her role of young mother, the Princess wears a pretty indoor cap with the strings left dangling behind her ears. Princess Maud wears a short lace-edged dress, the sleeves tied up with wide ribbons, and ankle-strap shoes with pompoms on the toes.

111 (left). *A vignette carte of Marie Alexandrovna, the wife of Queen Victoria's second son, His Royal Highness Prince Alfred, Duke of Edinburgh. He had travelled to St Petersburg in 1874 to marry the sister of the Tsar; she was also the grand-niece of the German Kaiser. The Duchess of Edinburgh was a serious young woman and in this carte, published shortly after her arrival in England, she wears a mid 1870s dress with a frilled neckline and yoke. She also wears a locket on a black velvet ribbon round her neck. This was a fashion in jewellery for the whole decade. Her head is dressed comparatively simply, for by the mid 1870s the top heavy coiffures with masses of false hair were going out of fashion.*

112 (right). *Her Royal Highness Princess Louise, Queen Victoria's fourth daughter, photographed in 1870, the year before her marriage to the Marquis of Lorne. This carte was taken by Hills and Saunders and published for public sale by Marion and Company. Like the Duchess of Edinburgh she wears a locket on a velvet band. Her dress has a low vee-neckline which is trimmed with a pleated frill on each side. The shoulders and front of the dress are veiled with a very pretty lacy scarf. She wears two bracelets; one, matching the velvet band at her neck, has a large round medallion on it; the other is a simple band, probably gold. Her hair is taken back from her forehead with a ribbon ornament pinned to the front, and is braided at the back. The photographer's setting is a rustic arbour.*

113 (left). *The Bishop of Manchester. A carte taken by Elliot and Fry in the 1870s. The Right Reverend James Frazer was an Oxford scholar with a lifelong interest in education and was the author of several books on the subject. He had served as rector in two large parishes in Wiltshire and Berkshire, as well as being Chancellor of Salisbury Cathedral, before being appointed Bishop in 1870. He is pictured here in his choir vestments. Over his black cassock he wears a white robe called a rochet, which is covered by the black sleeveless robe called a chimere. On top of this he wears a long tippet. His hat is a scholastic mortar board.*

114 (right). *Dugald Braidwood, Assistant Superintendent of the Edinburgh Fire Brigade, photographed in the late 1870s by Murray and Campbell, the successors to D. S. Hay at 68 Princes Street, Edinburgh. Although historically overshadowed by his older and more famous second cousin James Braidwood (first Captain of the London Fire Brigade Establishment), who was killed in the great fire of Tooley Street in 1861, Dugald was a popular and much loved figure in Scotland from the early 1860s onward — firemen were regarded as heroes by the Victorian public. As Assistant Superintendent he served under four Firemasters, finally retiring after thirty-eight years in service in 1893. He died the same year. In this carte he is shown wearing the dress uniform (worn on formal or ceremonial occasions), of the Edinburgh Fire Brigade. It was navy blue (possibly black) with black piping across the front of the sleeves and is based on a military uniform. The cap badge shows a pair of crossed axes with the city's name on the surrounding circle. The medal is the long service medal awarded after twenty years service, to which was added a bar for every five years. As Dugald Braidwood entered the Fire Service in 1855, this photograph must have been taken between 1875 and 1885. The epaulettes he is wearing are silver-coloured metal. The Firemaster may have had brass epaulettes while the ordinary firemen would not have worn them at all.*

115 (left). *Miss Bella Bilton, one of the leading beauties of 1890, was portrayed on a set of eight cartes, photographed by W. and D. Downey and published by the Photoglyptic Company. Cartes like this were intended for the collectors' market and Miss Bilton, who was part of a music-hall singing duo, with her sister Flo, is a classic example of an 1890s 'pin-up' girl, especially as she was the subject of a romantic Society scandal. On 10th July 1889 she married the young Lord Dunlo: they were both twenty years old. His father, the Earl of Clancarty, was so angry that, nine days after the wedding, he sent his son to Australia and, on his return, insisted that the young man petition for divorce. In court Lord Dunlo declared dramatically his belief in his wife's innocence, to the court's applause. Bella appeared in the pantomime 'Beauty and the Beast' at Christmas 1890, billed as 'Lady Dunlo'. After this performance she left the stage. Her father-in-law died six months later and she became the Countess of Clancarty, bearing her husband three children before her death in 1906, at the age of 38. In this carte she wears a glamorous version of the underclothes of the late 1880s — an embroidered chemise, a short tight wasp-waisted corset and a bunched and draped petticoat. Combined with loose hair and a fanciful cap, this gives a paradoxical impression of innocence and naughtiness.*

116 (right). *As a contrast, an earlier Victorian actress, born about 1850, Clare Rousby, known as 'the beautiful Mrs Rousby', was a gentle and graceful specialist in historical roles. In 1871, playing Joan of Arc in a play of that name, she rode on to the stage on horseback, wearing armour. The realism of this play, especially the death scene where real faggots were lit at the stake, caused much public protest. It did not, however, lessen her personal popularity. She was happily married to a fellow actor, Wybert Rousby, with whom she starred in many classical and Shakespearean roles. She died while still young and famous in 1879. This carte shows her soldier's costume as 'Joan of Arc'.*

THESE ARE THE LITTLE CHILDREN WHO CONVERT THE PARK RAILINGS INTO GYMNASTIC POLES, TO THE CONSTERNATION OF VOKINS'S HORSE!——

AND THIS IS ONE OF THE HYDE PARK KEEPERS HAVING HIS CARTE DE VISITE TAKEN.

[MORAL.   *Would it not be better if the Park Keeper attended to his duties a little?*

117. *A pair of cartoons by John Leach, published by 'Punch' in a book of 'Pictures of Life and Character' in 1869. The pictures show the clothes of the time in a simplified form, including the resplendent frock-coat uniform of the park keeper.*

photography shops and studios throughout Britain. Many family albums carried at least one photograph of a royal personage, and some families had separate albums for the faces of well known people. The commercially produced cartes included everyone who had ever made news. Would-be actresses and poverty-stricken beauties sold the rights of their picture to the commercial studios. Marion and Company were not the only wholesalers. S. Beale's list of celebrities of 1869 contains one thousand and nineteen names and subjects ranging from the Queen to 'Beauties of the Ballet'. The cost of each carte to the collectors was one shilling.

The working-class carte

Celebrities were not the only subjects collected by the Victorians, although they accounted for the bulk of them. But there was also a cult of the 'picturesque', and, alongside this, a great deal of serious research into social conditions. People interested in both these aspects collected cartes of working people in their working clothes. Most working-class women preferred to be photographed in their best clothes for their own family albums, particularly in the south-east of England. However, in the Midlands, north and west of England there were fewer inhibitions and some women themselves had their photographs taken in their working clothes.

The local photographers put copies of the photographs they had taken of local people in their shop windows along with the pictures of national celebrities. When they found that collectors wanted pictures of working folk, some photographers went out into the streets and fields, industrial works and seashores in search of suitably 'picturesque' subjects. Many of these photographs are the examples that can be found today of 'outdoor' cartes, and *Punch*, again, lampooned both the photographer in search of working-class subjects and the workers for letting themselves be photographed 'for a consideration'. Some of the photographers taking cartes-de-visite in the open air were itinerant workers themselves who travelled round the country villages creating a 'studio' in the open air by hanging up a sheet for a backcloth and putting a piece of old carpet down on the grass so that the unsophisticated country people could have a picture of themselves and their families.

One photographer whose pictures of local working girls were sold as curiosities was W. Clayton of Iron Street, Tredegar, Gwent. An album inscribed 'C. B. Crisp' in the photographic

118 (above, left). *Two elderly women photographed by a photographer from Helston, Cornwall, in the 1860s. They were probably photographed near their house, out of doors, the photographer using a sheet as a backcloth and placing a mat on the grass to form a 'studio'. The women may be sisters, or inmates of a charitable institution, for they are dressed alike, in plain dark dresses worn over crinoline petticoats, with fringed home-spun woollen shawls. They wear white caps with the lappets pinned up to look like ear muffs. The ribbons of the caps tie under their chins to make a bow hanging over their chests.*

119 (above, right). *A Guildford farmer of the 1880s, wearing a tweed jacket and trousers and carrying a bowler hat in one hand and a book in the other. A watch chain is looped over his waistcoat. This photograph was also taken out of doors.*

120 (opposite, left). *An estate worker, probably a gamekeeper, photographed in the 1870s by Gordon Thomas Allan from Ramsgate, Kent. He is wearing a shirt, corduroy trousers, a tweed waistcoat with wide revers and a round felt hat like a bowler with a flat brim. His laced boots would have been ankle-high. Most outdoors workers took off their jackets when at work, but he would have had a jacket similar to that in plate 75.*

121 (opposite, right). *Mr Peter Geesing, the coachman to the Gill family who lived in the mansion at Apps Court, Walton-on-Thames. This outdoor carte was taken by W. H. Deakin, the photographer from the nearby village of East Molesey, sometime between 1890 and 1895. The carte, which is now in the Weybridge Museum collection, was sent to one of the daughters of the Gill family in 1895, when Peter Geesing died, with the inscription 'In memory of a faithful friend and servant of your parents for sixty years'. He was eighty-seven when he died, so had presumably started working for the Gills when he was twenty-seven. He left a wife, a son (who was gardener to the Gills), a daughter who was a maidservant, and two grandchildren. The picture shows the old coachman in the garden, wearing a shirt, waistcoat, riding breeches and high boots. Men's waistcoats seem to have been made with the back in plain fabric since at least the seventeenth century; only the fronts are made in the fabric meant to match or contrast with the trousers and jacket with which they were worn. This carte shows the lighter fabric of the back of the waistcoat on the right shoulder and beside the right arm. The clothes pictured here would have been worn at work in the coach-house or stables. When driving he would have added a jacket or coat and a top hat.*

collection of the Gallery of English Costume in Manchester contains cartes by W. Clayton of the girls who worked on the slag tips. Some of these were taken in his studio, others out of doors, and all show the girls in their working clothes. C. B. Crisp, the collector, was obviously interested in the clothes of the girls, for a newspaper cutting pasted at the front of the album describes the ironworks and the slag heaps very briefly while the 'peculiar' dress worn by the women and girls is closely detailed. Their dresses and aprons, made of a cloth like fine sacking, were short — coming to just below the knee — showing knitted red stockings and heavy hobnailed boots. But it was the headgear worn by these girls that warranted the closest description. The writer was unable to decide if these objects were bonnets or hats for they were so shapeless, battered and dirty; nevertheless they were adorned with beads, brooches and feathers.

These girls, their conditions, their work and their clothes were the subject of protracted correspondence in the *Merthyr Telegraph*, and doubtless because of this the photographer persuaded the girls to pose for him knowing the cartes would sell. Some

122 (above). *Mine tip girls from Tredegar, South Wales. This carte is from the album collected by C. B. Crisp. The two girls wear the short-skirted dresses described on page 75. The short skirts reveal the heavy boots that were commonly worn by these girls. Their battered but decorated hats are worn over headscarves tied under the chin.*

123 (opposite, left). *A female collier from Rose Bridge pits, photographed on 10th August 1869 by Robert Little of Wigan. This girl wears trousers, boots, a short skirt (tucked up and sashed or belted round her hips), and a loose shirt made of a patterned, striped material. She is unusual in having nothing on her head. The pit-brow girls usually wore a bonnet made like a loose hood, padded across the front and tied behind the head.*

124 (opposite, top right). *Joanna, a milk woman from W. Stoats' Alderney Dairy of Upper Gloucester Place. She wears a short skirt, big apron and a large shawl. Another carte in the same collection shows this woman with her shawl over her head, pinned beneath her chin. The cartes were by Chamberlain of Marylebone, London, and taken in 1872.*

125 (opposite, bottom right). *Two fisher girls, Elizabeth Jenk and Fanny Scales, who wear their short skirts tied up at the knees to form breeches. This enabled them to climb up and down the cliffs to reach the beach to search for bait. Their aprons are tucked up at the waist and their dress sleeves are covered by long, light coloured oversleeves. Their bonnets, typical countrywomen's bonnets of the mid nineteenth century, are worn tipped well forward to shade their eyes. They were photographed in the studio of Walter Fisher of Filey, North Yorkshire, in 1871.*

126 (left). *A railway porter of the 1870s in corduroy trousers and sleeved waistcoat stands by a covered table in an incongruously rustic setting. Sleeved waistcoats were a survival from the early eighteenth century that had died out in fashionable dress by its second half. They survived in railway uniform to the late twentieth century, and in the nineteenth century were issued to station porters. They were made of corduroy with twill sleeves. Corduroy trousers were also uniform issue. Dark green was the colour favoured by many railway companies in the mid nineteenth century, although by the end of the century most were dark blue. This man is an employee of one of the Midland railway companies. With his uniform he wears a shirt with a turn-down collar and a narrow tie. His cap is of the type known as a 'cheese-cutter'. Although he is not wearing it in this picture, and would probably not have worn it for actual work, he would also have been issued with a cloth jacket to complete his uniform.*

127 (right). *A young employee of the North Eastern Railway, probably another porter, sits on a kitchen-type chair for his photograph. He wears corduroy trousers, a waistcoat with lapels and a short stand-up collar to his shirt. He had a broad tie and a watch chain and fob. His watch is in his waistcoat pocket, the other end of the chain being fastened through one of his waistcoat buttonholes. His jacket is single-breasted and of regulation cut. Both the jacket and trousers were probably dark (but not navy) blue. His cheese-cutter cap bears the initials NER. The carte is undated and has no trade plate on the back. It would appear to have been taken by one of the cheaper studios, with no background or fancy furniture, just a kitchen chair on the floor, which is covered by linoleum.*

collectors would commission photographers to take pictures of workers out of doors and in their studios. Others would stop workers in the street and take them to a photographer, paying both photographer and sitter, in order to add another carte to their collections.

One such collector was Arthur Munby, whose interest in working women, over a period of fifty years, has resulted in the diaries and photographs that now form the Munby Collection in the library of Trinity College, Cambridge. Munby, who started by being interested in working women simply as an observer, comparing them and their clothes to the fashionable women of his own middle class, became eventually a champion of the working woman and her right to work at any job she chose, and in doing so to wear suitable clothes and to have reasonable working conditions, wages and respect. His collection is a revelation of a fascinating background to the Victorian scene. His prose is clear, his descriptions unbiased and revealing, and the photographs destroy many preconceived ideas of Victorian England. He was particularly interested in the pit-brow girls of Wigan, and the photographs he collected show them working in trousers, shirts, aprons and bonnets, as healthy and uninhibited as any girl of today; yet other cartes in his collection show that on Sundays these same girls wore crinoline-supported dresses as decorously as any fellow-Victorian could have wished.

Other working women also wore clothes far removed from the fashionable norm and these, too, are revealed in cartes-de-visite from Munby's collections and elsewhere. Fisher girls in north-east England wore short skirts and turned them into breeches by pinning them round their knees while searching for bait on the shore. Fieldworkers or 'bondagers' also wore short skirts and distinctive bonnets. Possibly some collectors were attracted by the short skirts of these working women. When fashionable women hid their legs any woman's ankles or calves could become erotic. Female acrobats, whose pictures sold in vast quantities, wore even shorter skirts over tights. These worried Munby, for he considered their dress most unbecoming. There was, however, an enormous trade in pornographic cartes, some depicting women in various stages of undress, others nude. Munby hated this field of photography, finding it most offensive. He was interested in honest working women of all types, especially labouring women. He noted their clothes and liked to see them appropriately dressed for their job, even if their clothes were unusual and far removed from fashion. He deplored the servant girls who

128 (opposite, top left). *A young, priest of the Roman Catholic Church. This carte shows only his head and shoulders, emphasising his clerical collar. These round white collars, fastening at the back with a hinged stud, are still common to most Christian denominations' clergy. Even in Victorian times they were nicknamed 'dog-collars'. Over all his other clothes he wears a cassock with a stand-up round collar which is cut away in front to show the 'dog-collar'. The cassock would be long-sleeved and ankle-length. The triangular-crowned hat is called a biretta. The back of this carte is inscribed 'F. James Keating 1871'.*

129 (opposite, top right). *A Wesleyan Methodist minister, serving in a circuit in north Kent at the end of the nineteenth century. Methodist ministers are itinerant, moving on to a new circuit every few years, and so travelling round the country. Like the Roman Catholic priest (left) he wears a 'dog-collar'. However, he does not wear a cassock but a dark grey or black suit with a stand-up collar to his jacket. In place of an ordinary front-fastening waistcoat he wears a 'veststock', a waist-length upper garment covering only the front of his body. It fastens at the back of the neck and is cut away in front to reveal the collar. It is then cut to pass under the arms and fastens at the back at waist level. His moustache and steel-rimmed spectacles are typical of those worn by any professional man, such as a doctor, lawyer or schoolteacher, in the 1890s.*

130 (opposite, bottom left). *The Salvation Army was founded by William Booth — a former Methodist — in 1865. It was first known as 'The Christian Mission'. The evangelists wore suits of clerical cut with frock coats, tall hats and black ties worn with white shirts; they always carried a rolled umbrella with which to lead singing. When the name was changed to 'The Salvation Army' in 1878 it was decided that a military-style uniform would be appropriate, as would ranks within the organisation. They therefore pinned metal badges on their coats and hats. The ordinary members and the bandsmen wore blue guernseys or jerseys with 'Salvation Army' on the front. Blue ribbon bands, later red, with 'Salvation Army' on them were worn around hats or around the upper arm. Later the hats were standardised to army-type peaked caps. A uniform was designed in 1883, but it was not until 1887 that it could be purchased from the Salvation Army headquarters shop. As well as the cap, this uniform was of dark blue trousers and a Norfolk jacket with appropriate badges, including the well known 'S' badge on the upstanding collar. Women's uniforms were always similar but with skirts instead of trousers and a bonnet, especially designed by Mrs Catherine Booth, instead of the cap. This carte, taken in Pontypool, was photographed between 1878 and 1887.*

131 (opposite, bottom right). *An Anglican bishop of the 1860s in his outdoor clothes. He wears black knee breeches and buttoned gaiters with a short dark apron to cover the breeches. His collar is the normal clerical 'dog-collar' and his veststock is probably deep purple. Over this he wears a high-buttoning frock coat with a stand-up collar. His medium-high top hat is on the table beside him.*

occasionally borrowed their mistresses' clothes in which to be photographed.

Other champions of workers' or children's rights were also collectors of photographs, and photographs of workers, especially of women and children, were produced as evidence in many government enquiries into working conditions. Dr Barnardo took his own photographs of the waifs and strays he rescued, photographing them again newly clothed and in training as servant girls or young artisans. These pictures show clothes far removed from middle-class Victorian fashions.

Many working men, particularly railwaymen, sailors, soldiers and others whose work entitled them to a uniform, liked to be recorded wearing their uniforms. These cartes are portraits intended for family albums even though many of them may have

132 (above, left). *A Chief Petty Officer in the Royal Navy, about 1880. The photograph was taken by W. V. Amey of Commercial Road, Landport, Portsmouth. The uniform he wears is not unlike a modern petty officer's uniform, although the cut of the jacket is distinctively Victorian and very similar to the reefer-type jackets that were fashionable wear in the 1880s. The cap is smaller than a modern naval cap.*

133 (above, right). *A Victorian naval rating wearing a regulation loose blouse with the sleeves set in low on the shoulder. The seam on the left arm has a light-coloured stripe sewn into it, signifying he was a member of the port watch. (Naval crews were divided into two 'watches', one half being on duty, the other below; they were designated 'port' and 'starboard' watch.) This picture was taken by George Nesbitt of Bournemouth, who claimed he was patronised by the Prince and Princess of Wales. The only official visit of the Prince and Princess to Bournemouth was in 1890. As the 'watch' stripe was abolished from naval uniform in 1895, this photograph must have been taken between 1890 and 1895. Note his cap has no cap tally with his ship's name on it; the Victorian sailor wore a soft cap with no stiffened rim to it. Nineteenth-century seamen were not issued with clothes, but fabric to make them. Many made their own clothes, including the caps. Some enterprising sailors earned extra money by making their shipmates' clothes for them.*

134 (opposite, left). *A British Army private of 1890 from a rifle unit. He wears a plain dark tunic fastened with seven brass buttons and a belt with a plain double-loop fastening. His regimental badge is worn on his collar, on each side of the front fastening. His sleeves are trimmed with dark braid and his hat is a plain 'pillbox' whose strap rests under his lower lip, not under his chin.*

135 (above, right). *A slightly later carte from Aberystwyth, showing another private. He is a member of a volunteer battalion of a line infantry regiment and his uniform is more ornate. The edge of his jacket is bound with white and he has white cuffs and braid on his sleeves, a white collar and a broad white canvas belt with a large crested buckle. Army regulations stated that all white parts of uniforms were to be kept white by brushing off any dirt and then applying 'blanco' (a solution of pipeclay) which dried quickly to leave a white coating on any surface to which it was applied. Belts, collars and cuffs were so treated while buttons and badges were of brass and would need to be polished. His cap is a forage cap decorated with brass buttons and his regimental badge.*

been collected by others. Some of the men in these photographs were obviously very proud of their occupations.

Not all the people who posed for cartes-de-visite in their working clothes were artisans. Clergymen are one example of these; naval and army officers are others. Bishops or generals may, perhaps, be classed as famous people, but the cartes of many of their lower-ranking fellows are now examples of men in particular callings, and no doubt were collected as such by their fellow Victorians. Many families with sons in military service made collections of cartes of fellow officers or men, and these are

136 (left). *This carte of a young working man is also an advertisement for his employer.
Charles Vickery of Hastings, Sussex, was in business as a cook and confectioner from the
1830s to 1861, when he died. His business was taken over by Miss Ann Maria Lock, who
was employing three men at the time of the 1871 census. This presumably is one of the men.
Possibly his work was to deliver the products, hence the box with the name of the business
on it; certainly he is wearing outdoor clothes. The reefer-type jacket and shallow-crowned
hat are those that could have been worn by a worker when not actually engaged in manual
work (for which the jacket would have been removed) or as casual middle-class wear. The
studio setting and the fact that Vickery's name is on the box suggest that the photograph was
taken in the early 1860s. The photographer was H. Clasby.*
137 (right). *If Ann Lock was enterprising in having her employee photographed, even more
enterprising was Sidney Webb, the photographer who took this picture of a girl in Welsh
costume. Born in the 1830s in Bristol, by 1861 he was a licensed victualler in Pembroke. By
1869 he was describing himself as an 'artist' and by 1878 he was a photographer, officially
appointed to the Admiralty in Pembroke Dock. In the 1880s he went back to being a
publican, running the 'Prince of Wales' inn in Laws Street North, Pembroke Dock. During
the 1870s he posed this attractive young woman in the clothes of a South Wales cockle-seller.
The fishing basket and the dress with its quilted petticoat, jacket bodice, Welsh woollen
check apron and oversleeves are authentic working dress, but the hat and cap are fancy dress
and the girl herself is too elegant to be a fisherman's wife. Pembroke was becoming*

fashionable as a holiday resort at the time, and a carte such as this would have been a collectable souvenir in the days before picture postcards became common.

138 (left). *Equally collectable from the Victorians' point of view would have been this carte of a little Indian prince taken by Elliot and Fry of London. Its date could be any time in the nineteenth century, although the pale sepia tones of the original and the large column beside the child suggest the 1860s rather than a later date. The child wears an elaborately embroidered tunic, trousers and cap, and may or may not have been a real Indian prince. Like the Welsh cockle-seller the clothes, genuine or not, may have been worn as fancy dress.*

139 (right). *'Fancy balls' or fancy-dress parties were a popular diversion. Many women's magazines and pattern books published designs and ideas for fancy dress and there were recognised characters, often in romanticised versions of working costumes. This woman, whose dress is cut in the basic style of the 1870s, represents an itinerant broom-seller. Real broom-sellers were desperately poor tinkers, making and selling small brooms from the bushes on commons. This outfit is nothing like the real clothes of such a person, but it would have been instantly recognised as such by the seasoned Victorian fancy-dress party goer.*

Window & Grove.   Baker Street.
MISS GERARD.
Permanent Photo.   COPYRIGHT. Waterlow & Sons Co.

now excellent source material for military and naval uniform enthusiasts.

National costumes are another aspect of the Victorian collector's field. Scottish, Welsh and Irish photographers were quick to publish 'typical native dress' cartes. These not only showed the sitter's choice of costume but could also be sold to travellers and curiosity hunters. Murray and Campbell, whose studios were at 68 Princes Street, Edinburgh, advertised on the backs of their cartes in the early 1880s: 'Ladies photographed in Fishwife Dress and Gentlemen in Highland Dress. Dresses for the above styles kept on the premises.' As the British Isles have no true national costumes — apart, perhaps, from the Scots — these cartes, while somewhat theatrical, are still very much of their own time and the clothes depicted reveal Victorian fashionable details while pretending to be 'traditional'.

140 (opposite). *In Victorian times, as now, manufacturers realised that by associating their products with popular and beautiful people they might increase sales. This carte was one of a series featuring actresses issued by Taunus Table Waters in the 1870s. Miss Gerard wears an idealised and somewhat theatrical version of current 1870s fashions. Men may have collected these cartes for the beauty of the actresses pictured on them, but many women in the provinces would have used the cartes as a guide to fashion, although few would have worn as low-cut a dress as this without a chemisette or a modesty piece to fill in the neckline. This carte comes from the album of the Goldsmith family of Hastings (page 64).*

141 (below, left). *Dr Barnardo was a great believer in the power of photography and sold cartes of children in his care to raise funds for his work. The cartes were sold in packs of twenty for five shillings, or singly for sixpence each. They all had impassioned appeals on the back, as here. Dr Barnardo was accused of misrepresentation in selling these cartes. At an arbitration court he pointed out that 'when first found, the children were often in dark or very confined places, and in any case were so dirty, verminous or even injured, that they needed attention straight away. To photograph them in those conditions would be inhumane. In any case, the advertising cartes were sold to raise funds and represented the types of children saved, and what could be done for them, rather than specific children.' Like all advertising it was slightly overstated to produce the desired effect.*

142 (below, right). *One of Dr Barnardo's cartes that were sold to raise funds for his work. This picture shows a child in rags and barefoot. His clothes are a mixture of child and adult clothing and it would not have been odd to see children so clothed in many large cities in the nineteenth century. The companion to this picture shows the same boy clothed in a much better fitting, and whole, shirt and trousers, working with tools at a bench. While many of Dr Barnardo's early 1860s photographs were taken on the street at the time he found the children, once he had realised the power of advertising the pictures used for that purpose were posed in the studio and the boys 'dressed up' in rags for the purpose.*

East End Juvenile Mission,

HAVING DEPÔTS IN

STEPNEY, LIMEHOUSE, AND RATCLIFFE,

LONDON. E.

UNDER THE HONORARY DIRECTION OF

DR. T. J. BARNARDO.

THE above MISSION was established by its present Director in September, 1866, or nearly eight years ago. Its aims are to rescue the *Destitute* and *Neglected* Boys and Girls continually found wandering, homeless and friendless, throughout the great Metropolis, and to bring them under the sheltering influences of kindly and well-regulated "HOMES."

In these Homes the children are educated and taught various branches of Industry; but, above all, are carefully instructed in the Word of God, the Director and his co-workers being increasingly assured that the secret of a radical reformation is to be found alone in a TRUE CHANGE OF HEART.

These Photographs are sent forth at the request of many kind friends, who had already obtained one or two single copies in a more private manner, but desiring a collection of them, suggested the publication of the present series. We earnestly hope that the view of the bright, or, it may be, the sad faces of our young protégés will lead the friends who purchase the Photographs to sympathize very truly with us in our happy but sometimes deeply trying labours.

THE HOME FOR
WORKING AND DESTITUTE LADS,
18 & 20, STEPNEY CAUSEWAY. E.

E. E. J. M.

Home for Working & Destitute Lads.

NO. 27. *ONCE A LITTLE VAGRANT.*
(*The same lad as on card No. 28.*)

143 (top). *A carte commemorating the opening of the Holborn Viaduct on 6th November 1869. Both the omnibus company and the photographer are advertised in this photograph. The driver, Thomas Grayson, wears a smart chesterfield overcoat and a low-crowned top hat. The lower half of his body is protected by a waterproof apron. The conductor wears a baggy overcoat and a bowler hat and has a large money-bag slung over his shoulder.*

144 (bottom). *The reverse of the card advertises the photographer again and also the driver of the omnibus, who owned the copyright of the carte.*

Advertising cartes

There was more than disinterested public service behind the willingness of photographers to produce novelty cartes for the collector market. As most cartes carried the photographer's trade plate on the back, every carte sold, either to a sitter or a collector, was another advertisement for the photographer. It was not long before other manufacturers realised this, and by the 1870s cartes carrying advertisements were not uncommon. A series of cartes carrying the portraits of actresses was sponsored by a mineral water company. Transport companies issued advertising cartes of their vehicles for sale to passengers as souvenirs. Achievements and events, from Queen Victoria's Golden Jubilee to the opening of bridges, were commemorated in cartes-de-visite.

Shopkeepers would have themselves photographed in their doorways, or small manufacturers would have their staff photographed with the tools of their trade or with a box with the name of the firm on it. Dr Barnardo's 'before and after' photographs of the children he cared for were not only records, but also advertisements for his work and the children's home, and were sold to raise funds for it. The popularity of cartes-de-visite with collectors made them an ideal medium for advertisements in Victorian times: today they provide excellent documentation of social and fashion history.

Tailpiece

The end of the nineteenth century was also the end of the cartes-de-visite. Although a few provincial studios did continue to produce cartes-de-visite into the beginning of the twentieth century, they, and the larger but similar cabinet prints, were a manifestation of the Victorian age. As such, they recorded our forebears posed in all their variety and show us their attitudes, their faces and their fashions *à la carte*.

In the twentieth century our improved technology has enabled the studio postcard portrait and the family snapshot to record all this and more, and these will surely delight future historians as much as the cartes-de-visite do us.

4. Further reading

Costume books

Cunnington, C. Willet, and Cunnington, Phillis. *English Costume in the Nineteenth Century*. Faber and Faber, 1966.

Cunnington, Phillis, and Buck, Anne. *Children's Costume in England*. Adam and Charles Black, 1966.

Ewing, Elizabeth. *History of Children's Costume*. B. T. Batsford, 1977.

Fischel, Dr Oskar, and von Boehn, Max. *Die Mode*, volume 5 (1843-78). F. Brukman AG, Munich, 1910 (reprinted 1920s and 1930s).

Taylor, Lou. *Mourning Dress*. George Allen and Unwin, 1983.

Tozer, Jane, and Levitt, Sarah. *Fabric of Society*. Laura Ashley, 1983.

Costume and photography books

Ginsberg, Madeleine. *Victorian Dress in Photographs*. B. T. Batsford, 1982.

Hiley, Michael. *Portraits from Life*. Gordon Frazer, 1979. (The diaries and photographic collection of A. Munby.)

Wheatcroft, Andrew. *The Tennyson Album*. Routledge and Kegan Paul, 1980. (A photographic biography.)

Photography books

Dimond, Francis, and Taylor, Robert. *Crown and Camera*. Penguin, 1987. (The Royal Family and photography 1842-1910.)

Hannavy, John. *The Victorian Professional Photographer*. Shire, 1980.

Heyert, Elizabeth. *The Glasshouse Years*. Allenheld and Schram/ George Prior, USA, 1979.

McCanley, Elizabeth Ann. *A. A. E. Disderi and the Carte-de-visite*. Yale University Press, 1985. (Portrait photography.)

Wagner, Gillian, and Lloyd, Valerie. *The Camera and Dr Barnardo*. Dr Barnardo School of Printing, Hertford, 1974.

Wall, John. *Directory of British Photographic Collections*. William Heinemann Ltd, 1977.

Wills, Camfield, and Wills, Deirdre. *The History of Photography*. Hamlyn, 1980.

Various authors. *Punch in Cameraland*. Focal Press, 1948.

145 (left). *A photograph showing the blouse and skirt which were almost a uniform for young women at the beginning of the twentieth century. Striped blouses like this appear time and time again in the last cartes-de-visite. Here the woman wears a wide stiff belt fastened with heavy silver clasps to define a neat waist. This too is almost universal. Necklines are high, but the masculine type of tie which had been fashionable in the 1890s is giving way to a softer-style scarf. This carte is from the studio of Valery, of Beckenham, Kent.*

146 (right). *'April 2nd. 1904. Fred on Nellie's Wedding Day' is the inscription on the back of this carte by A. Hopkins of Dartford. It shows a young man in an Edwardian lounge suit, stiff collar and leather gloves, sitting astride a cottage-type chair. Though we may never know who he was, in this picture he is serene and confident, captured by the camera on one of the last of the cartes-de-visite.*

5. Places to visit

Most local museums and record offices have fairly large collections of photographs relating to their own districts. Many have albums of cartes-de-visite that belonged to local families. However, they will probably not be on show, and visitors will have to ask to see them, and in some cases make an appointment to see them. Similarly, some museums that specialise in costume will also have photographs, but these will probably be used for reference rather than display. There are several museums that now specialise in photographs and a list is given below together with a selection of local museums with photographic collections. There are many more than those listed here. Although all these museums have cartes-de-visite there is no guarantee that they will be on display, but it should be possible to make an appointment to see them. They are listed in alphabetical order.

Banbury Museum, 8 Horsefair, Banbury, Oxfordshire. Telephone: 0295 259855.

Blackburn Museum and Art Gallery, Museum Street, Blackburn, Lancashire BB1 7AJ. Telephone: 0254 667130 or 680603.

The British Photographic Museum, Bowden House, Totnes, Devon. Telephone: 0803 863664.

Elmbridge Museum, Church Street, Weybridge, Surrey KT13 8DE. Telephone: 0932 843573.

Gallery of English Costume, Platt Hall, Rusholme, Manchester M14 5LL. Telephone: 061-224 5217.

Liverpool Museum, William Brown Street, Liverpool L3 8EN. Telephone: 051-207 0001.

The Minories Art Gallery, 74 High Street, Colchester, Essex CO1 1UE. Telephone: 0206 577067.

Museum of London, London Wall, London EC2Y 5HN. Telephone: 071-600 3699.

National Centre of Photography (Royal Photographic Society of Great Britain), The Octagon, Milsom Street, Bath, Avon BA1 1DN. Telephone: 0225 462841.

National Museum of Photography, Film and Television, Prince's View, Bradford, West Yorkshire BD5 0TR. Telephone: 0274 727488.

National Portrait Gallery, St Martin's Place, Trafalgar Square, London WC2H 0HE. Telephone: 071 306 0055.

Scottish National Portrait Gallery, 1 Queen Street, Edinburgh EH2 1JD. Telephone: 031-556 8921.

Staffordshire County Museum, Shugborough, Stafford ST17 0XB. Telephone: 0889 881388.

Strangers' Hall Museum, Charing Cross, Norwich, Norfolk NR2 4AL. Telephone: 0603 667229.

Tiverton Museum, St Andrew Street, Tiverton, Devon EX16 6PH. Telephone: 0884 256295.

Victoria and Albert Museum, Cromwell Road, South Kensington, London SW7 2RL. Telephone: 071-938 8500.

Viewpoint Photographic Gallery, Vulcan House, The Crescent, Salford, Greater Manchester. Telephone: 061-737 1040.

Welholme Galleries, Welholme Road, Great Grimsby, Humberside DN32 9LP. Telephone: 0472 242000 extension 1385.

Welsh Folk Museum, St Fagans, Cardiff, South Glamorgan CF5 6XB. Telephone: 0222 569441.

Woodspring Museum, Burlington Street, Weston-super-Mare, Avon BS23 1PR. Telephone: 0934 621028.

Acknowledgements

The author wishes to convey her thanks to the following, without whose help the book could not have been written: Arthur Gill, Chairman of the Historical Group of the Royal Photographic Society, who made available the fruits of his own research into cartes-de-visite and provided cartes from his collection for inclusion; James Fenton, of the Fenton Photography Museum, for his advice and encouragement and the loan of cartes for inclusion; Mrs M. Reynolds, great great grand-daughter of John Mayall, who allowed a choice of her own collection of Mayall cartes; Mrs Pamela Haines, Local Studies Librarian of Hastings Central Library, for her family album and history; Martin Russell, of Kingston Camera Club; Philip Daniell and John Rotheroe, who collected cartes to aid research (some are included in the book); the many friends and colleagues in museums, record offices, libraries and other organisations who answered questions and identified pictures, especially Robin Bryant of the Salvation Army, Miss Frances Dimond of the Royal Archives, Bob French of the Southern Veteran Cycling Club, Dr Timothy Hobbs of Trinity College, Cambridge, and Ian McMurtrie of the Braidwood and Rushbrook Museum; lastly, but by no means least, Mrs Marion van der Voort, who donated her family album and typed all the text, and Howard Lansdell, Honorary Secretary of the Historical Group of the Royal Photographic Society, and photographer extraordinary, who has done as much work on this book as the author and without whose support and aid it would never have been finished.

The author is grateful to Colin and Grace Osman for their help in revising the further reading list (chapter 4) for the second impression.

Photographs are acknowledged as follows: Dr Barnardo's, 141, 142; Fenton Photographic Museum, 49, 109, 110 and page 4; Arthur Gill, 19, 22 (both), 143, 144; Miss K. M. Gill, 121; Mrs Pamela Haines, 9, 101, 102, 103, 104; Mrs Lorna Hart, 54; Manchester City Art Gallery, 122; *Punch*, 6; Mrs M. Reynolds, 4, 5, 21, 36, 131; Martin Russell, 126, 132; Trinity College, Cambridge, 123, 124, 125; Mrs Marion van der Voort, 55, 77, 97, 98, 99, 100; Weybridge Museum, 15, 27, 56, 72, 76, 79, 88, 90, 93 (photograph by Jack Chinn), 117 (both), 119, 134. All other cartes are from the author's collection.

Index